WORKING WITH ANGER

Also by Thubten Chodron

Buddhism for Beginners

Cultivating a Compassionate Heart: The Yoga Method of Chenrezig

Don't Believe Everything You Think: Living with Wisdom and Compassion

Good Karma: How to Create the Causes of Happiness and Avoid the Causes of Suffering

Guided Meditations on the Stages of the Path

How to Free Your Mind: The Practice of Tara the Liberator

Open Heart, Clear Mind: An Introduction to the Buddha's Teachings

An Open-Hearted Life: Transformative Methods for Compassionate Living from a Clinical Psychologist and a Buddhist Nun

Taming the Mind

Books edited by Thubten Chodron

Choosing Simplicity: A Commentary on the Bhikshuni Pratimoksha, by Ven. Bhikshuni Master Wu Yin

Transforming Adversity into Joy and Courage: An Explanation of the Thirty-seven Practices of Bodhisattvas, by Geshe Jampa Tegchok

www.thubtenchodron.org
www.sravastiabbey.org

WORKING WITH ANGER

Buddhist Teachings on Patience,
Acceptance, and Transforming Negativity

THUBTEN CHODRON

SHAMBHALA

Shambhala Publications, Inc.
2129 13th Street
Boulder, Colorado 80302
www.shambhala.com

Cover art: Yuravector/Shutterstock and Pupahava/Adobe Stock

9 8 7 6 5 4 3 2 1

Printed in the United States of America

Shambhala Publications makes every effort to
print on acid-free, recycled paper.
Shambhala Publications is distributed worldwide by
Penguin Random House, Inc., and its subsidiaries.

Library of Congress Cataloging-in-Publication Data
Names: Thubten Chodron, 1950– author.
Title: Working with anger: Buddhist teachings on patience, acceptance, and
    transforming negativity / by Thubten Chodron.
Description: Boulder: Shambhala Publications, 2024. | Includes
    bibliographical references.
Identifiers: LCCN 2024003334 | ISBN 9781645472889 (pbk.: 2024 ed.) | ISBN
    9781559391634 (pbk.: 2001 ed.)
Subjects: LCSH: Anger—Religious aspects—Buddhism. | Patience—Religious
    aspects—Buddhism. | Compassion—Religious aspects—Buddhism. |
    Religious life—Buddhism. | Buddhism—Doctrines.
Classification: LCC BQ4430.A53 T48 2024 | DDC 294.3/44—dc23/
    eng/20240202
LC record available at https://lccn.loc.gov/2024003334

CONTENTS

PREFACE

Anger plagues all of us on a personal, national, and international level. When it manifests in the mind of even one person, let alone a group or nation, the entire world can be affected—witness the two world wars of the last century. On a personal level, anger can destroy our relationships with the people we value the most and keep our mind bound in spirals of misery. Within groups, anger splits people into factions and sets people striving for a common beneficial aim at cross-purposes to each other. In the international arena, anger fuels the conflicts in the Middle East, the Balkans, and elsewhere.

As powerful as anger is, it lacks any material substance whatsoever. Nevertheless, it can drastically affect our lives and the lives of others. When we look into our own minds and hearts and understand this disturbing emotion better, we will recognize its unrealistic projections and thus will not buy into its story so readily. We will gradually be able to distance ourselves from this painful emotion, without suppressing, repressing, or expressing it. We will replace it with more wholesome and beneficial states of mind, and in this way, patience, tolerance, love, and compassion will grow within us. Learning the techniques for doing this is the purpose of this book.

Working With Anger is written for everyone, because no matter what our education, socio-economic class, gender, race, or religion, we risk falling prey to anger's clutches. Written in informal, friendly language, this book includes numerous examples of daily life situations in which these teachings may be applied. Some of the examples were told to me by friends, family, and students, while others are from my own life.

Overview

Chapter one sets the stage by introducing the Buddhist view of mind, emotions, and anger. From there, we will define anger and discuss its disadvantages in chapter two. Chapter three speaks of patience—the antidote to anger—the ability to remain calm in the face of harm and suffering. The fourth chapter considers remaining doubts we may have of the benefits of subduing anger and developing patience, while the fifth discusses repressed anger and factors prompting the arisal of anger in our mind.

Chapter six begins the description of techniques to counteract anger, and chapter seven continues this by illustrating creative ways to handle the hurt and anger that arise when we are criticized. Chapter eight shows us how to avoid blaming ourselves or others for our problems and have a broader perspective. It also deals with the anger that arises due to being physically ill. Each of us has buttons—sensitive points and issues—which, when accidentally or intentionally pushed, throw us into a tizzy. How to work with these situations is considered in the ninth chapter.

Accepting the present reality of situations—yet working to improve the future—is a powerful antidote to anger and the topic of chapter ten, while chapter eleven identifies our self-centeredness as our real enemy and describes the unusual techniques of giving our suffering to our self-centeredness and seeing the kindness of the person who harms us. Grudges and resentment can weigh on us as we collect them over the years. Letting go of these so that we can go through life with a happy heart is the topic of chapter twelve. The thirteenth chapter deals with the painful issue of the betrayal of trust, while the fourteenth gives us ways to handle the snake of envy.

Sometimes our anger focuses not on others, but on ourselves, and we become caught in chains of guilt and self-blame. Letting go of these is the topic of chapter fifteen. Cultivating love and compassion enables us to prevent anger from arising, and gaining wisdom eliminates it from the root. These topics are discussed in chapters sixteen and seventeen respectively.

While most of this book deals with how to handle our inner emotion of anger, appendix one discusses external behaviors—various conflict styles—and with which motivations and in which circumstances they can be employed. A glossary and a list of recommended reading are also included at the end of the book for your use.

My wish is that this book contributes to harmony in our world—the harmony that each of us longs for in our own hearts and the harmony that we wish to create among each other in societies. I believe that it is not survival of the fittest that enables a species to continue to exist, but survival of the compassionate. My teacher, His Holiness the Dalai Lama, often points out that ants and bees cooperate much more with each other than we supposedly more intelligent human beings. On its own, an ant would perish, but caring about and cooperating with others, it lives and prospers.

When our minds are joyful and free from anger and resentment, we work and share with others to the advantage of all, while when we are miserable and angry, we sabotage others' good work as well as our own. This is very clear when we think about it: No one wakes up in the morning and says, "I feel so happy today. I think I'll go out and hurt someone!" We only harm others when we are tormented by anger. Being the interdependent creatures that we are, our destructive behavior triggers the same in others. Thus, the way to stop the cycle of suffering depends on each of us working with our own anger in constructive ways and cultivating our compassionate heart that wishes others well.

Working with Anger is based on teachings of the Buddha, the wise, compassionate teacher who lived in India in the sixth century BCE. In subsequent centuries, great Indian sages commented on the Buddha's teachings, as did practitioners in each country to which Buddhism spread. Due to the kindness of my teachers, I have heard these instructions and now have the opportunity to share them with you. Through putting them into practice, we will experience the benefits.

All errors in this presentation are my own.

The Origins of this Book

As a Buddhist nun and teacher, I am often asked to give talks on working with anger. The beginnings of this book were based on two talks I gave on this subject—one at Evergreen Buddhist Association in Kirkland, Washington, in 1989, and the other at a Buddhism and Psychology Conference at the University of Washington in Seattle, in 1992. Based on these, a booklet entitled "Working with Anger" was published for free distribution by Amitabha Buddhist Centre in Singapore. Because people were enthusiastic about this topic, that booklet was enlarged and made into this book.

Appreciation

I would like to thank my teachers—especially His Holiness the Dalai Lama, Tsenzhab Serkong Rinpoche, Zopa Rinpoche, and Geshe Ngawang Dhargye—for their supreme patience in teaching me the Dharma. They shared with me the priceless teachings of the Buddha, the Indian sages Shantideva and Dharmarakshita, and the Tibetan practitioners Tsongkhapa and Togmey Sangpo, from whose texts the material in this book is drawn. In addition, my teachers' living example of patience and compassion has inspired me to have confidence that these teachings, when put into practice, have the potential to eradicate anger and create harmony. My own small attempts to practice patience have reconfirmed this.

Many thanks also to Dharma Friendship Foundation for supporting me while I worked on this book. Cindy Felis transcribed the original tapes, and Laurie Rostholder, a psychotherapist, made many valuable suggestions. Barbara Rona, a most competent editor, worked far beyond the call of duty to shape and refine the manuscript. I am very grateful for her help.

And, as Zopa Rinpoche taught me, instead of being angry with the people who have harmed me, I must express my gratitude to them, for they are kinder than the Buddha, and without their help I will not attain enlightentment. May all positive energy generated from this book go towards the temporary and ultimate happiness of each and every living being.

Thubten Chodron
Seattle, WA
February 24, 2001

Chapter One

MIND, EMOTION, AND ANGER

One summer His Holiness the Dalai Lama spoke to a Los Angeles audience that included a group of inner city youth in fatigues—their camp uniforms—together with their counselors. After his talk, one of the youths asked His Holiness, "People get right in my face and provoke me. How can I not fight back?" She was challenging him, but quite sincere in her request.

His Holiness looked her in the eye and said, "Violence is old-fashioned. Anger doesn't get you anywhere. If you can calm your mind and be patient, you will be a wonderful example to those around you." The audience clapped, but the girl remained standing, looking back at him. She wasn't yet satisfied.

The Dalai Lama went on to describe how so many great people—Martin Luther King, Mahatma Gandhi, and Jesus, for example—remained peaceful in the face of violence and adversity. Many of them experienced difficulties when they were growing up. "Even me," he said. "My youth was fraught with conflict and violence. Yet all of these people expounded non-violence and love for others, and the world is better for their contributions. It's possible for you to do this too."

He then motioned for the girl to come up and shake his hand. As she approached him with her hand out-stretched and a nervous smile on her face, the Dalai Lama opened his arms and hugged her. The girl returned to her seat, beaming.

After the talk, one of the sponsors asked the teenagers if they would share their experience. A burly, tough-looking young man came to the microphone with a huge smile on his face. "Phew," he said, "You must be able to hear my heart beating from where you're sitting! I've seen the Dalai Lama on TV and in the magazines and thought he was pretty cool, but I just can't describe what it feels like to have met him!" and he touched his heart.

A Tibetan monk who had escaped from communist-occupied Tibet just a few years earlier told me his story. His family was a wealthy, prominent one in the area of Tibet where he grew up. After the communist occupation of Tibet in 1950 and the subsequent abortive uprising in 1959, his family's house was confiscated and made into a jail. Because his family were landowners and because he was a monk, he was arrested by the Chinese communists. Then, he was imprisoned in a jail that had once been his home. He and the other inmates were allowed to go to the toilet outdoors twice a day, but otherwise they had to stay in the house, which now had broken windows and none of its former comforts. Most people would have burned with rage at the injustice and humiliation, but this monk told me that he tried to use his time wisely, doing his meditation practices to improve the state of his mind. Although he was deprived of all his religious implements, he silently recited the texts he had memorized and contemplated their meanings. In this way, he familiarized his mind with attitudes and emotions that lead to enlightenment and avoided the pitfalls of anger. When I talked with him, I detected no sign of resentment against the Chinese communists. He had a profound love of life.

Stories such as these lead us to wonder, "How do they do it?" They are human beings just like us, and although they have faced circumstances much worse than a great many of us have faced—including exile, imprisonment, torture, and the loss of many loved ones—they do not burn with rage or seek revenge. This book is largely a collection of Buddhist methods for subduing and preventing anger that have worked for the Dalai Lama, the monk above, and many others.

There is nothing particularly "Buddhist" about these methods. In fact, many of the Buddha's teachings are common sense, not religious doctrine, and common sense is not the property of any religion. Rather, these methods show us reasonable and beneficial ways to live. No matter what our religion, looking at our minds and learning to work with our anger are helpful.

Buddhism has been called a science of the mind, and many of those who practice it say the Buddha was similar to a great therapist who taught practical methods for dealing with disturbing attitudes, negative emotions, and daily life problems. Buddhism, of course, goes beyond the scope of psychotherapy and differs from it in some significant ways. Nevertheless, like psychology, it deals with the human mind and emotions and strives to create happier human beings and a better society.

Although we may wish to immediately dive into the practical applications for anger management, these are presented within the context of a Buddhist view of mind and emotions. Thus some background on this topic will help us understand them.

The Buddhist Perspective on Mind and Emotions

The term "mind" refers to the experiential, cognitive, intellectual, perceptual, and feeling part of us. It is non-material in nature, while our body, made of atoms, is material. Within the broad category of mind, we find many types of mind. Among these are sense consciousnesses—which perceive external objects such as sights, sounds, smells, tastes, and touches—and our mental consciousness, which thinks, dreams, sleeps, and can experience spiritual realizations.

Anger, like all emotions, is a type of mind. It is a mental factor that accompanies our conceptual mental consciousness. Thus, it may be affected—either subdued or inflamed—at the mental level. Patience, love, compassion, and joy are similarly mental factors that accompany our mental consciousness, albeit not at the same time as anger. They, too, can be enhanced or diminished at the mental level. For this reason, the Buddha emphasized that our mind is the source of our suffering and happiness.

The word "mind" may also be translated as "heart," as in "that person has a kind heart." Here we see that Buddhism does not make the same distinction between thinking and feeling that we make in the West, where we believe that thought is conceptual and emotions are not. Indeed, Sanskrit, Pali, and Tibetan—all languages in which Buddhist texts are written—have no word which is a direct translation of "emotion." From a Buddhist perspective, many emotions, such as anger, have a feeling component but are conceptual, for they know their objects by means of a mental image. For example, we can be angry when the person at whom we are mad isn't even in the room. At that time, we are not perceiving the person with our eyes, but we are thinking about him in that a mental image of him appears to our mind.

What is Anger?

In Buddhism, anger (Tibetan: *khong khro*) is a mental factor that, being unable to bear a person, object, situation, or idea, harbors ill will towards it or wishes to harm it. Anger covers a range of emotions including annoyance, irritation, frustration, spite, belligerence, resentment, hatred, and rage. Although the English word "anger" may very occasionally be used in a positive sense, here, as one of the root disturbing emotions, it has only a negative meaning.

The forerunner to anger is a mental factor called inappropriate attention that, in this case, exaggerates the negative qualities of a person, object, situation, or idea or projects onto it negative qualities that are not there, thus creating an incorrect story about it. For example, Dave walks into the office one morning and his colleague, who is preoccupied, doesn't greet him. He thinks, "This person is unfriendly and rude," and based on this inappropriate attention that projected meaning and motivation onto the other's action, he becomes irritated. His internal irritation leads to external action, and Dave makes a sarcastic remark, which hurts his colleague, and she, in turn, snaps back at him. We can easily see how one instant of inappropriate attention and anger can set off a chain reaction of events causing ourselves and others misery.

At a meeting of His Holiness the Dalai Lama and Western scientists to discuss destructive emotions, I learned that scientists in general delineate three components of emotions: the feeling, the physiological, and the behavioral. For them, the meaning of "anger," then, includes not simply a feeling, but also the physiological activation of particular areas in the brain and the release of certain hormones in the body. In addition, it includes the behavior, such as shouting or sulking, that accompanies a particular instance of anger.

Buddhists, however, refer primarily to the feeling component when they speak of emotions such as anger or compassion. Buddhist texts contain little discussion of the brain or of hormones, probably because the scientific instruments for detecting their functions are recent developments. Anger is related to the body—to the energy in our body as well as to the hormones, such as adrenaline, which influence it—but anger itself is not a physical state. It is a mental one, although some people first know they are angry by recognizing physical indications such as muscle tension or a churning stomach. Also, for Buddhists, the meaning of "anger," or other emotions, does not include the behavior that accompanies a particular instance of the emotion.

Negative Emotions and Freedom from Them

Western culture and Buddhism have varying meanings for "negative emotion" and "positive emotion." For Westerners negative emotions are ones that feel bad, and positive emotions are ones that feel good. Sadness, for example, is a negative emotion because the person feels deflated, whereas attachment to a beautiful house is a positive emotion because the person feels happy.

From a Buddhist viewpoint, however, the distinction between positive and negative emotions depends on whether they lead to cyclic existence or to liberation. Cyclic existence is the constant recurrence of the problems we face from one life to the next as a result of our fundamental ignorance. Liberation is freedom from this, a state of lasting happiness. Thus certain types of sadness may be positive, for example, the sadness we feel when we realize that sense objects cannot bring us lasting happiness. This sadness is positive, because being disillusioned with something that cannot bring lasting happiness leads us to generate the determination to be free from cyclic existence and attain liberation. On the other hand, although it may feel good, clinging attachment to possessions, such as our house, is considered harmful because it keeps us tied to cyclic existence. With such attachment, we repeatedly seek happiness from external sources—people and things that, just like us, are transient and therefore unable to provide us with enduring happiness. Buddhism teaches methods for subduing destructive emotions, those that keep us in cyclic existence, and methods for developing constructive emotions, those that lead us to liberation.

The Possibility of Change

Subduing negative emotions and cultivating positive ones is possible because, according to Buddhism, we do not have a fixed, solid personality. What we label "I" is related to our body and mind, both of which are constantly in a state of change. Physically, the subatomic particles of our body are constantly in flux, and mentally, our perceptions, moods, thoughts, and emotions continuously change. Since change is happening every moment, our challenge is to guide it in a productive way.

Enlightenment does not entail a total makeover of our personality—some Buddhas may be introverted and others extroverted, some may prefer Mexican food and others Italian food. However, enlightenment does entail letting go of certain aspects of our personality—the habitual emotions and attitudes that keep us trapped in a prison of our own making. Abandoning these completely is possible because they are not an inherent part of our mind.

The basic nature of our mind is often compared to the clear, open sky. The sky is always there although some days it is obscured by clouds. However, the clouds are not the nature of the sky, so they can be eliminated. Similarly, the disturbing attitudes and negative emotions such as anger are not the nature of our mind and may be abandoned, leaving the radiant and pure nature of the mind.

In addition, the disturbing attitudes and negative emotions are based on ignorance. In this case, "ignorance" doesn't mean, for example, not knowing the capitals of each nation. Rather, it is a particular type of ignorance, that which, unaware of the nature of reality, conceives people and phenomena to exist inherently, with their own independent essence. When ignorance is eliminated, all the harmful mental factors depending on it vanish, in the same way that once a tree is uprooted, its branches also die. Since ignorance misapprehends reality, it can be abandoned by seeing reality correctly. The mental factor that does this is called wisdom, and for this reason, Buddha's teachings speak extensively about cultivation of the wisdom that realizes the lack—or emptiness—of inherent existence.

Before we are able to use wisdom to cut destructive attitudes and emotions at their root, we must rely on easier methods to counteract them. For this reason, great Buddhist masters, such as Shantideva, talked of a variety of easy-to-use "antidotes" to anger, techniques to neutralize this poisonous emotion. Most of this book consists of these techniques.

Chapter Two

THE DISADVANTAGES OF ANGER

Anger may give us a tremendous sense of power, but at the same time it undermines the happiness of ourselves and others. As Gedundrup, the First Dalai Lama, said in a prayer to the female Buddha, Tara:

> Driven by the wind of inappropriate attention,
> Amidst a tumult of smoke-clouds of misconduct,
> It has the power to burn down forests of positive potential,
> The fire of anger—save us from this danger!

Is Anger Accurate in Its Assessment of Reality?

Anger is inaccurate in its assessment of reality because, by definition, it is based on exaggeration or superimposition of negative qualities. However, when we are angry, we don't feel that we're exaggerating or superimposing anything. We feel that we're right! In fact, the angry mind seems to be very clear: "I'm right. You're wrong. You need to change."

Under the influence of anger, we select a few negative details and form a limited view that we are then reluctant to change. For example, Diana worked in the same organization as Harry, and although she didn't know him very well, they supported the same goals. One day he canceled a workshop she was scheduled to give, and feeling that his action had been unfair, she was angry. For months, every time she saw him or heard his name, something tightened inside her. Then it occurred to her that, based on a half-hour of this person's forty-five year life, she had formed an opinion of who he was that she was certain was correct. "Surely," she realized, "he is much more than this one unfortunate encounter we had." Seeing that her anger was inaccurate, she let go of her fixed opinion of him. Since Diana no longer scowled at him, Harry became friendlier to her and eventually they were able to discuss and resolve the cancellation of her workshop.

Holding onto and nurturing a fixed, inaccurate opinion of someone breeds suspicion and continual unhappiness. When we are mad at someone, everything he does appears wrong, and we take even the simplest act as more evidence that our negative view of him is correct. In the above example, every time Harry made eye contact with Diana and greeted her, she thought he was ridiculing her, taunting her because he had more power. In fact, he knew she was upset and was trying to create a friendly space in which he could talk with her about what had happened.

Psychologists speak of a refractory period that accompanies an emotion. During this time, we are closed to any advice or reasonable interpretation that contradicts our view. We can neither think clearly about a situation nor accept other interpretations of it that well-meaning people offer. The refractory period may be short—just a few seconds—or it may last years and even decades. When the emotion subsides and we are able to look at the event more clearly, we readily see, as Diana did, that anger's interpretation was inaccurate.

Anger is also inaccurate in its assessment of reality in that it does not perceive a situation in a balanced way, but views it through the distorted filter of "me, I, my, and mine." Although we think that the way a situation appears to us is how it really exists out there objectively, when we are angry, we are, in fact, viewing it through the filter of our self-centeredness. For example, if the manager criticizes my colleague, I may not get angry. In fact, I may even console my colleague by saying, "Don't take what the boss said personally. It's not a big thing. He's under a lot of pressure and is just venting. It doesn't have anything to do with you, and he'll be different tomorrow." But if the manager criticizes me, I will likely be upset. The situation appears extremely serious to me. I dismiss anything my friends might say and dig myself more deeply into a hostile hole. Actually, no difference exists in the words the manager said to my colleague and to me. Why, then, am I upset when he looks at me while speaking, but not when he looks at my colleague? Because it's me, and as much as I don't like to admit it, I feel that what happens to me is much more important than what happens to anyone else.

Due to this ingrained, self-centered view, anything that happens in relation to me seems incredibly important. I spend my time thinking about my problems, not anyone else's (that is, unless I'm attached to that person). People could be starving in the world, my neighbor could be undergoing a horrible divorce, and another colleague could be diagnosed with cancer, but after cursorily acknowledging their misfortune, I get down to the real crisis: the criticism I received. This may initially seem a trite or flippant description, but if we observe what we spend our time thinking about, we'll see that our problems, our life—everything related in one way or another to me —takes first place.

Is Anger Beneficial?

We generally consider something beneficial if it promotes happiness. But when we ask ourselves, "Am I happy when I'm angry?" the answer is undoubtedly no. We may feel a surge of physical energy due to physiological reasons, but emotionally we feel miserable. Thus, from our own experience, we can see that anger does not promote happiness.

In addition, we don't communicate well when we're angry. We may speak loudly as if the other person were hard of hearing or repeat what we say as if he had a bad memory, but this is not communication. Good communication involves expressing ourselves in a way that the other person understands. It is not simply dumping our feelings on the other. If we scream, others tune us out in the same way that we block out the meaning of words when someone yells at us. Good communication also includes expressing our feelings and thoughts with words, gestures, and examples that make sense to the other person. Under the sway of anger, however, we neither express ourselves as calmly nor think as clearly as usual.

Under the influence of anger, we also say and do things that we later regret. Years of trust built with great effort can be quickly damaged by a few moments of uncontrolled anger. In a bout of anger, we treat the people we love most in a way that we would never treat a stranger, saying horribly cruel things or even physically striking those dearest to us. This harms not only our loved ones, but also ourselves, as we sit aghast as the family we cherish disintegrates. This, in turn, breeds guilt and self-hatred, which immobilize us and further harm our relationships and ourselves. If we could tame our anger, such painful consequences could be avoided.

Further, anger can result in people shunning us. Here, thinking back to a situation in which we were angry can be helpful. When we step out of our shoes and look at ourselves from the other person's viewpoint, our words and actions appear differently. We can understand why the other was hurt by what we said. While we need not feel guilty about such incidents, we do need to recognize the harmful effects of our uncontrolled hostility and, for the sake of ourselves and others, apply antidotes to calm it.

In addition, maintaining anger over a long time fosters resentment and bitterness within us. Sometimes we meet old people who have stockpiled their grudges over many years, carrying hatred and disappointment with them wherever they go. None of us wants to grow old like that, but by not counteracting our anger, we allow this to happen.

Some people interpret Buddhist teachings on the disadvantages of anger to mean that we're not supposed to become angry, or are bad and sinful if we do. The Buddha never said this. No judgment is involved. When we're angry, the anger is just what is at that moment. Telling ourselves we should not be angry doesn't work, for anger is already present. Further, beating up on ourselves emotionally is not beneficial. The fact that we became angry doesn't mean we're bad people. It just means that a harmful emotion temporarily overwhelmed us. Anger, cruel words, and violent actions are not our identity. They are clouds on the pure nature of our mind, and they can be removed or prevented. Although we are not yet well trained in patience, we can gradually develop this quality when we try.

Two Stories

We can notice in our lives the adverse effects of behavior motivated by anger. As *The Dhammapada* says:

> Avoid speaking harshly to others,
> Harsh speech prompts retaliation.
> Those hurt by your words
> May hurt you back.

An ancient story aptly illustrates this. Once there was a king who ruled a great kingdom in India. He enjoyed a happy life, except that his young son would often quarrel with the ministers, servants, and other family members. Everyone found the son's behavior unbearable, yet no one dared complain to the king. After some time the king himself saw what was happening and sought help. He employed the best therapists, but they could not subdue the boy's behavior, nor could the local sports heroes, miracle workers, and entertainers. In fact, the child's behavior became more obnoxious.

One day a monk came to the town to collect alms. The king's messenger observed him walking gently and mindfully and asked him to come to see the king. The monk, who had high spiritual realizations, declined this opportunity for riches and glory, saying " I am no more bound to the worldly life and therefore have nothing much to discuss with a king in the world."

Hearing of the purity of the monk's mind, the king went to pay homage to him and asked if he needed anything. The monk said that he simply wished to stay in the nearby forest, to which the king responded, "That is my forest, so please live there without worry. We will bring you food daily and will not disturb your meditation. I ask only that you allow me to bring my son to visit you. He is a big troublemaker and I'm at a loss as to what to do with him." The monk nodded in consent.

The next day the king and his son arrived at the royal forest in a chariot. The king returned to the palace, while the monk and the boy walked in the forest. Suddenly they came across a small neem tree, and the monk asked the prince to pluck a leaf and taste it. The boy did so and spit out the bitter leaf in disgust. He bent over and force-fully grabbing the young tree by its trunk, uprooted it.

The monk said to him, "My child, you knew that if this sapling were to continue, it would become a huge tree, which would be even more bitter in the future. For that reason, you plucked it out. In the same way, the ministers, royal officers, and palace residents now think, 'This young prince is so bitter and angry. When he grows up he will become even more vicious and cruel to us.' If you are not care-ful, they will pluck you from the kingship as soon as they can." Un-derstanding the disturbance he was inflicting on others and its ramifications for himself, the prince decided that he must change his attitude and behavior. Although it required effort, he knew it was for the happiness of all, and as he changed, others ceased their negative reactions to him and came to love and respect him.

In a more modern episode, Floyd told me of his outbursts of road rage. Once, while he was driving on the highway with his fiancee, another driver cut him off. Infuriated, he sped up, overtook the other car, and deliberately lurched in front of it. At such speed, he lost con-trol of the car. It skidded across three lanes and skimmed an embank-ment before finally coming to a halt. He suddenly realized that his rage had almost killed his fiancee and deep remorse overcame him. He then stopped interpreting others' poor driving as a personal af-front. Who knows how many lives have been saved by his change of attitude?

Chapter Three

PATIENCE: THE ALTERNATIVE

Because anger and other destructive emotions are not the nature of our mind/heart, they can be diminished and eventually removed completely from our mindstream through the development of patience, love, compassion, and wisdom. Many of the people we admire—the Buddha, Jesus, Mahatma Gandhi, and others—had the ability to remain internally undisturbed in the face of harm and externally act for the benefit of others. Their anger was neither expressed nor supressed. It was simply absent, having been transformed into tolerance and compassion.

Thus, an alternative exists to either expressing or supressing anger. When we express our anger, our words and deeds can easily hurt others. In addition, expressing anger does not rid ourselves of it. On the contrary, each time we express hostility—even if it is by beating a pillow or screaming in an empty field—we strengthen the habit of feeling and acting out its violent energy. What happens if one day no pillow is around to beat and no field nearby in which to scream and we are surrounded only by human beings? On the other hand, supressing anger doesn't eliminate it either. It may still erupt, sometimes when we are least prepared to handle it. Also, suppressing anger may damage us physically or mentally. Expressing anger is one extreme, and suppressing it is another. In both cases, the habit of anger remains in one form or another.

Patience is an alternative. It is the ability to remain internally calm and undisturbed in the face of harm or difficulties. The Sanskrit word *"kshanti"* has no suitable equivalent in English. Here we use "patience," but "kshanti" also includes tolerance, internal calm, and endurance. Thus "patience," as it is used here, also includes these qualities.

Patience does not involve pasting a plastic smile on our face while hatred simmers inside. It involves dissolving the anger-energy so that it is no longer there. Then, with a clear mind, we can evaluate various alternatives and decide what to say or do to remedy a situation.

In speaking of both patience and anger, we must differentiate mental attitudes from external actions. Patience may manifest in various behaviors. It gives us the mental space to choose appropriate behavior for a situation. Sometimes we may speak strongly to others because that is the most effective way to communicate with them at that moment. For example, if a child is playing in the street and her father gently says, "Susie dear, please don't play in the street," she will likely ignore him. On the other hand, if he speaks forcefully, she will more likely remember and obey. But internally, his mind can be calm and compassionate when doing this. The child will sense the difference between the words said when he is centered and the same words said when he is upset.

In other situations, a patient attitude may manifest as calm behavior. Rather than retort to a passerby's taunt, Bob chooses not to respond. He does this based not on weakness or fear, but on the wise decision not to feed a potentially hostile situation.

Similarly, anger may manifest in different behaviors. When Gary is angry, he explodes. He shouts, curses, and at times has even been known to throw something. Karen, however, withdraws. She goes into her room, closes the door, and refuses to talk. She may sulk for days. These two people are both angry, but they manifest it in totally different behaviors: one is aggressive, the other passive.

The Advantages of Patience

A common misconception in the West is that patience equals passivity. However, when we correctly understand the meaning of patience—noting that it is an internal attitude, not an external behavior—we see that this is incorrect. Rather, calmness in the face of harm gives us the space to evaluate situations clearly and thus to make wise decisions. This is one of the foremost advantages of patience.

Another advantage of patience is that it benefits our health by leaving our mind free from turbulence and pain and our body free from tension. Many studies show that calm people heal more quickly after surgery and are less likely to have accidents. Ronda, upset by a conflict with a neighbor, was hammering together a new cabinet with ferocity. Suddenly she pulled herself up and thought, "If I continue like this, I'll certainly hurt myself." She breathed deeply, let her physical tension go, and resumed her carpentry with a different attitude.

Patience also enables us to live free from the pain of grudges, resentment, and the wish for revenge. Because we are then able to communicate better with others, our relationships are more harmonious and last longer. Instead of their being ripped apart by anger, they are deepened by attentive listening and considerate speech. We thus amass fewer regrets, so our mind is at ease at the time of death. Accumulating positive karma, we know we are on the path to fortunate rebirths, liberation, and enlightenment.

Patience, in addition, directly affects the people and atmosphere around us by short-circuiting the dysfunctional ways in which people interact with each other. Following are three stories illustrating this.

Before school, Ron's daughter arrived at the car frustrated because her hair band was tangled in her hair. Instead of scolding her for doing her hair at the last minute and thus condemning them both to a bad day, Ron smiled and helped her pull out the band.

Air rage—screaming at an airline employee over delayed or canceled flights—is common in our society. We vent our animosity on strangers not responsible for our misery and powerless to do anything about it. Because I travel to teach in various places, I am well accustomed to hassles due to weather, mechanical difficulties, or overbooking. On an especially long trip from the West Coast to the Middle East, one flight after another was beset with problems. Knowing I could do nothing about it, I relaxed and smiled at the people around me. Later, a fellow passenger, whom I did not know, came over and said, "Watching how you handled this helped me calm down, and I feel better. Thank you."

A number of prisoners with whom I correspond are turning around their lives through learning the Buddha's teachings. One of them told me the following story:

"Yesterday, I was heating up a cup of coffee and noticed, off to the side, a guy who frequently acts a little crazy. He mumbled as I walked past with my coffee, so thinking he might have been speaking to me, I stopped and calmly asked what he had said. 'I'm talking to myself,' he responded, so I started to walk away. But before I had taken two steps, he screamed, 'What! Can't I talk to myself?'

"I really dislike confrontation, but remaining calm, I said, 'I asked only because I thought you might be talking to me. I never said you couldn't talk to yourself.' He was excited by now and sternly faced me and said, 'You're nobody. You should get to steppin'.' I agreed that I was nobody special, smiled, and walked away.

"Knowing that this could mean trouble, I went to my room, put on my boots, and prepared as best I could for whatever he might do. I relaxed a little and looked back at what had happened—I had only spoken to him briefly once or twice before and hadn't done anything to upset him, yet he was obviously irate. I recalled karma, as nothing else seemed to make sense, and thought that I must have created the causes for this to be happening. I decided he probably had mistaken my question and felt threatened, or maybe he was already upset, or perhaps he had forgotten to take his medication. Reflecting on *The Eight Verses of Thought Transformation* helped me remain thoughtful and calm.

"I wasn't mad at him, although I was prepared to defend myself if necessary. I went to where he lived, meaning to talk to him and calm him down, but at the last moment, thought the better of it and figured he just needed to be alone. Later that day, he apologized and explained, 'I'd had an argument with someone else and was worked up. I wasn't in a very good mood when you came by.' I accepted his apology.

"Later, I reflected on how I had dealt with the situation. Not only did I refrain from verbal and physical violence, but also I even recalled the Dharma in the middle of it. I'm not saying this to boast, but I actually surprised myself. The situation could have erupted into violence and trouble, so I was very grateful for the help the Dharma gave me."

Chapter Four

IS ANGER EVER USEFUL?

Some people see advantages to anger. How true are their claims? Unless we find them to be false, we will not be motivated to transform our anger. It's crucial, then, to investigate one by one the claims about the advantages of anger to see if they are valid.

A Reliable and Necessary Detector of Wrongdoing?

Many years ago, I met with a group of specialists in the field of mediation and conflict resolution. As I spoke about the disadvantages of anger, these professionals became tense and eventually angry, until one blurted out, "Anger is necessary and beneficial because it gives us information about what is wrong!" Their argument was that our anger lets us know that another's behavior is not acceptable. Without it, they claimed, we could not discriminate just from unjust, acceptable from unacceptable.

However, anger is not a reliable or necessary indicator of wrongdoing. We may become angry not because our rights have been denied, but because we did not get what we wanted. We may become angry not because someone's behavior is unacceptable according to basic societal and ethical standards, but because we are hypersensitive. And even if someone has violated our rights or gone beyond conventionally acceptable etiquette or protocol, anger is not necessary to signal that the other has been inappropriate. With a clear and calm mind, we can assess the situation and reach the same conclusion. Indeed this latter method of detecting wrongdoing is a more beneficial method than anger, since it has none of the adverse side effects of anger discussed previously.

Although anger is not a reliable, necessary, or beneficial source of information for detecting wrong, it does let us know that our mind is disturbed and that our buttons are being pushed. Rather than acting according to our habitual pattern of blaming others for our anger, we can note that our buttons being pushed depends on two factors: others' actions and our having buttons. If we remove our buttons, there won't be anything for others to push! Of course, doing this requires a lot of internal work on our part.

By removing our buttons, we do not eliminate our ethics and values. Rather, we change the automatic and habitual responses that so often get us tangled in cycles of anger and conflict with others.

A Good Antidote to Vulnerability, Guilt, and Self-Blame?

Is anger a good antidote to feelings of vulnerability, guilt, and self-blame, for example, in cases of child abuse, rape, or divorce? When we're angry we may have the energy to state, "What this person did to me is wrong!" As strange as it sounds, our ego may find comfort in being angry: "I know who I am now. I am a victim of abuse, rape, or injustice." When we have a sense of being a victim, though, we also have a sense of being dependent on others for our inner peace. Thus, once we have acknowledged that another has harmed us, we must be alert to any anger tied to this discovery.

Initially, we may feel vulnerable if we let go of the "protective" shield of anger. Fears abound: "My anger is justified. If I give it up, who will I be? Isn't it tantamount to admitting what the other person did was right? How can I feel self-dignity without being outraged at what others have inflicted on me?" When angry, we may feel a sense of power, but this is false power because, fueled by aversion and blame, anger needs an enemy to exist. Genuine self-confidence, on the other hand, is open and lacks defensiveness. It is based on knowing our great human potential and the fundamental purity of our mind, not on others acting in any particular way.

To heal, we must grow beyond resentment and blame, arriving at a state of peace and acceptance in our heart, where we are willing to let the past be past and to go on with our lives with vitality and compassion. Such healing involves a process that takes time and patience with ourselves. It cannot be rushed or forced.

How can we release our anger in cases of abuse and mistreatment—whether at the personal, community, or international level? One way is to acknowledge and accept our anger, along with the pain and fear that propels it, and to note that all of these are mental events—temporary feelings that arise in our minds but do not define who we are. In Buddhism, we practice observing the arising, abiding, and disappearing of such mental factors without either rejecting the feelings or letting them overwhelm us. Whether we reject a feeling or become attached to it, the result is similar—that emotion controls us. When we can allow an emotion to be, without either pushing it away or buying into its storyline, it will gradually lose its power over us. Feelings dissipate by themselves because they are transient by their very nature.

An Essential for Winning at Sports?

The sports enthusiast claims that anger helps us win the game. But is it beneficial to focus on winning? Is it worthwhile to reinforce a negative characteristic just to get a trophy? Our minds become very tight when we make "us versus them" too concrete. "*My* team must win. We have to fight and beat the enemy." Why? "Because my team is best and that's because it's mine." Of course the other team feels the same way. Who is right? Competitive sports may be a socially accepted way of venting anger, but they don't cure the anger. They only temporarily release the physical energy accompanying anger, and in fact, may breed more hostility. We're still avoiding the real problem, our misconceptions of people and situations.

Can athletes be excellent without being fueled by the energy of anger? Yes. They can concentrate on doing their best rather than on winning. Then, win or lose, they'll have the satisfaction of developing their skills and enjoying the physical exercise, camaraderie, and team spirit.

If this sounds impractical for the tough world of sports, consider the story of Coach John Wooden, told by Brian Biro in *Beyond Success* (Pygmalian Press, 1995). "John Wooden remains the most acclaimed college basketball coach in the history of the National Collegiate Athletics Association (NCAA). In his final twelve years at UCLA, his teams won a staggering total of ten NCAA Championships. No other coach has won more than four" (p. xii). Yet winning was never the goal of Coach Wooden and his UCLA Bruins. It was only the by-product of their true focus. Indeed, "John Wooden never used the word 'winning.' He believed winning was not in his or his players' control. Instead, he constantly instilled his definition of success within himself and his teams... 'Success is peace of mind that is a direct result of self-satisfaction in knowing you gave your best effort to become the best of which you are capable'" (pp. 34-5). Fueled, then, not by anger, but by industriousness and enthusiasm, the two cornerstones of his system, Coach Wooden's teams achieved consistent excellence. "'No building is better than its structure,' he said, 'and no one is better than his or her mental foundation'" (p. 57).

A Protective Biological Response?

Some people claim that everyone naturally and automatically experiences anger in reaction to harm. It is "hard wired" into us biologically. Anger contributes to the survival of our species, for it enables us to defend ourselves effectively. Without it, we would stand by and let ourselves or our dear ones be harmed. In fact, anger, competition, and proving one's might over others have been indispensable evolutionary tools to ensure survival of the fittest. Of course, they say, sometimes angry behavior gets out of hand, so the real question is not how to eliminate anger, but how to express it appropriately, to the correct person, at a suitable time.

While from a certain perspective, the above argument makes sense, Buddhism has a different viewpoint. The species that prosper the most, it says, are those in which cooperation is the strongest. For example, a single ant cannot live on its own. If ants within one colony expended most of their energy battling each other, they would soon self-destruct. They need each other to survive, and they cooperate with each other extensively. Spend some time watching an ant colony. The ants scurry back and forth carrying building materials and food many times their own weight. They signal to each other where to go so that no one gets lost, and they work together to ensure the survival and prosperity of the group.

Similarly, we humans have difficulty living on our own. In the twenty-first century, we are more dependent on one another than in any other time in human history. Hundreds of years ago, people grew their own food, sewed their own clothing, and constructed their own dwellings. Now, the vast majority of people in developed countries do not know how to do these tasks for themselves. We need each other to survive, thus making cooperation imperative. Sometimes despite our human intelligence, these tiny ants seem much saner and more clever than we!

Since Darwin, the belief in the virtues of angry self-defense and competitive trouncing of one another has gained acceptance in many areas of society, including education, the arts and sciences, sports, computer development, and national defense. I believe the adoption of this paradigm has been extremely damaging for our world, resulting in a lack of compassion that allows humans to harm each other and their environment.

A certain kind of "competition" is good—not with other living beings upon whom our survival and happiness depend, but with our own ignorance and uncaring attitudes, which are our real enemies. We can generate the motivation to improve ourselves and our world because we care about them, not because we want simply to come out on top.

While the threat of harm may prompt a biological response, this response is not necessarily beneficial, nor is it innate within human beings. As mentioned above, anger originates with the inappropriate attention that interprets events in a distorted way. The body then produces adrenaline. With the mind as the motivator and the body as the cooperative condition, violent behavior then erupts. On the other hand, when the ignorance that supports anger is eliminated through the application of appropriate antidotes, these responses do not occur in the mind, and the vicious cycle halts. When we eliminate the distorted mental factors that bind us, our relationship to our body and our life changes. We can still protect ourselves and others from danger, but we do so without antipathy towards the harmer. In fact, a mind free from anger can more quickly find a good solution.

A Positive or Necessary Motivator for Social Change?

Although anger may energize us to prevent or correct social injustice, it cannot be counted as a positive motivator for social change, because it renders our minds like the minds of those whom we oppose. As a student, I saw this quite clearly at a Vietnam War protest, where another student picked up a stone and threw it at the ROTC building. Although I was not yet a Buddhist, I recoiled at this person's action. He had become just like the people against whom he was protesting.

No matter what the cause, when we hate the oppressors, our mind becomes like theirs. Both they and we are angry. Both of us consider our position right and the other's wrong. Both have a hard time listening to the needs and interests of the other party. Both think the other should change. When we approach conflict with such self-righteous indignation, communication, cooperation, and the willingness to compromise break down.

Is anger the only motivation that can energize us to correct harmful situations? According to Buddhism, it is not. Compassion—the wish for others to be free from difficulties and confusion—is not only a powerful motivator, but also one that is more balanced, realistic, and effective than anger. Although we may initially react in anger to injustice, by applying the techniques described in the following chapters, we can transform our attitude to a more compassionate one before acting.

For many years, I have lived in the Northwest part of the USA, where deforestation is commonplace. When it occurred near a retreat center our spiritual community regularly used, witnessing the deforestation was particularly painful, and some retreatants were hostile whenever a logging truck drove by. But a bumper-sticker saying "Hug a logger instead of a tree" made me think, "The loggers want to be happy and avoid suffering just like the deer they are displacing and the retreatants who miss the forest. Many of them probably do not like their work. I may disagree with the policies of the companies who employ them, but I don't need to hate either the CEOs or the loggers." Although I continued to sign anti-logging petitions and oppose deforestation, I began to wave to the loggers who drove by. Why not? They smiled and waved back.

We sometimes confuse compassion with passivity, sentimentality, or Pollyanna idealism. From the Buddhist perspective, it is none of these. Compassion is an attitude which realizes that others' wish to be happy and to avoid difficulties is just as intense and worthy of respect as our own. Others may be confused and use harmful methods in their endeavor to be happy. That has to be remedied. But their wish for happiness is to be honored. If we can see that both the victim and the perpetrator of harm equally want to be happy and free from suffering, we can intervene to stop harmful situations with compassion for both sides, not compassion for the victim and vengefulness for the perpetrator.

In 1989, a journalist asked His Holiness the Dalai Lama, "After the massive destruction the Chinese communist government has wreaked on your country and people, why aren't you angry? How can you tell the Tibetan people to have compassion for their oppressors?" His Holiness responded, "What good would it do to be angry? If I got angry, then I wouldn't be able to sleep at night or eat my meals peacefully. I'd get ulcers, and my health would deteriorate. My anger couldn't change the past or improve the future, so what use would it be? However, with compassion we Tibetans can act to improve the situation."

A Better Choice than Forgiveness?

Sometimes we feel that forgiving the people who have harmed us is tantamount to condoning their harmful behavior. Therefore, staying angry with them seems the only way to express our continued disapproval of their behavior. However, this isn't the case at all. A person and his behavior are separate. We cannot say that a person is evil even if his behavior or intention is harmful. From a Buddhist perspective, each being has the innate potential to become a fully enlightened Buddha. Each person has some internal goodness that can never be destroyed, no matter how badly he or she may act. Thus, we can forgive and let go of our anger toward the person who harmed us and at the same time maintain that his behavior was injurious and unacceptable and should not be continued in the future.

Forgiving does not mean tolerating damaging behavior or staying in an abusive situation. Nor does it necessitate sharing our forgiveness with the other person if he could misconstrue it and resume his harmful behavior. Motivated by compassion, we can take strong measures to prevent or interrupt harm. Thus, forgiving does not render us a "softy."

Forgiving benefits ourselves as well as others. When we hold onto our anger, we're tense and unhappy, and this affects our relationships and physical health. By forgiving, we let go of our anger and thus cease our own suffering. We also prevent ourselves from assuming the role of the perpetrator, as victims so often do, and thus we stop the cycle of harm.

Of course we cannot force ourselves to dissolve our anger or to forgive someone. Sometimes we first may need to remove ourselves physically from a stress-provoking person or situation to get some mental distance. Then, through practicing the antidotes to anger, we can gradually dissolve it. As we do, the spaciousness, clarity, and gentleness of forgiveness will naturally arise in our hearts.

For example, for years Trudy had been angry with her mother for neglect and abuse she experienced as a child. As she grew older, Trudy realized that this anger interfered with her ability to feel compassion and love for others. Under the guidance of a therapist and a spiritual teacher, she worked hard to overcome her anger, and to accept and forgive her mother. She also made an effort to be more loving and kind in her other relationships. While Trudy was working on herself, her mother was apparently doing the same. Much to Trudy's surprise, one day her mother called to express regret for her behavior, and asked for Trudy's forgiveness. Trudy gave it, feeling happy for both her mother and herself.

One of the most poignant meditations I have ever led occurred at a retreat in Israel, following a discussion of the Holocaust. A Jewish woman had shared her experience of attending a gathering of children of Holocaust survivors and children of Nazis. When she listened to the SS officers' children talk, she came to understand the deep guilt, suffering, and confusion they carry. How can one reconcile the memory of one's loving father with the knowledge that he sanctioned the murder of millions of human beings?

Then we meditated on Chenresig, the Buddha of Compassion. We imagined Chenresig in the concentration camps, in the gas chambers, and in the trains and prisons. We visualized Chenresig in Auschwitz, in Dacau, and in the other camps. As we recited the compassion mantra, *om mani padme hum,* we imagined the brilliant light of compassion radiating from Chenresig and permeating every atom of these places and of the people in them. We imagined it purifying the suffering, hatred, and misconceptions of all the beings—Jews, political prisoners, gypsies, Nazis, ordinary Germans who turned a blind eye to save their own skin—and healing all their pain. We chanted the mantra together for over half an hour, and the room was charged. Seldom have I meditated with a group that was so concentrated.

People wonder whether forgiving means forgetting. No, it does not. Remembering is important, but no benefit comes from keeping the pain, hurt, resentment, and anger alive in our hearts. Remembering with compassion is more powerful.

Chapter Five
RECOGNIZING OUR ANGER AND ITS CAUSES

Sometimes our anger seems to come out of nowhere, and we explode quickly. Other times, we feel that anger is lurking under the surface in some repressed form that influences our life. How can we learn to recognize when we're angry? What factors cause it to arise? The answers to these will help us to be aware of and understand our anger which, in turn, will facilitate transforming it through practicing patience.

Recognizing We're Angry

Before we can transform or eliminate our anger, we must be able to identify it. While sometimes our anger is self-evident, other times we don't recognize that we're annoyed, irritated, hostile, or belligerent until those emotions are strong and we are speaking or acting aggressively. This may happen for a variety of reasons. For example, we may be distracted by the external environment and out of touch with our own feelings; we may deny our anger because we think it's bad; or we may know something is the matter, but not know what it is.

For some people recognizing and labeling their anger takes training and practice. There are several ways to learn to identify it. For example, while meditating on the breath, we can observe what distractions arise that take us away from the object of meditation. We may recognize a general feeling of restlessness or anger, or we may remember a situation from years ago about which we are still irritated. By becoming familiar with the emotional tone and "flavor" of the various emotions subsumed under anger, we will learn to identify and label them: irritation, frustration, spite, jealousy, resentment, rage, belligerence, hatred, and so forth. Of course, we also have many positive emotions such as equanimity, love, compassion, and joy, but these seldom turn up as distractions in our meditation.

Another way to identify anger is to note our physical sensations. For example, if we feel our stomach tighten, jaws clench, or heat surge in our body, it could signal that we are becoming angry. Each person has different physical manifestations of anger, and we need to observe and note what ours are. Doing this is helpful, for sometimes it's easier to identify the physical sensations accompanying anger than the anger itself.

A further way to identify anger is to observe our moods. When we're in a bad mood, we can pause and ask ourselves, "What is this feeling? What has happened to prompt it?" Sometimes we can observe patterns in our moods and behaviors. These can give clues as to how our minds operate and to what our anger clings. For example, Mark noticed that he is in a bad mood almost every morning when he wakes up. Knowing this, he informed his roommates, and instead of engaging with people right away in the morning, he does his meditation practice. Breathing meditation allows his bad mood to dissipate, and if he is angry about a specific situation, he then works with his anger in one of the ways we will discuss.

Repressed Anger

Some people in therapy speak about repressed anger, meaning they still resent something from the past, but are not aware that they are angry. In therapy, a client may need to tap into and initially express anger in a safe situation with the therapist. By acknowledging the anger, he can then proceed to apply the antidotes to it. However, when trying to get in touch with anger, a person must take care not to fuel the anger or create anger that wasn't there. I remember a young man at a workshop trying to speak in an angry tone because his therapist had suggested he might have repressed anger. Although he was trying to clench his fists and scowl, it was apparent that he wasn't really angry. Rather, he was trying to feel something that he thought he should feel, given what had happened to him. I believe he would have benefited from relaxing and simply observing what he did feel, instead of assuming that he had anger he couldn't feel.

Some people speak of repressed anger as if they thought they were angry all the time but did not know it. They have the image of anger being actively present in them, under the surface all the time, ready to explode outward. Such a self-image can be harmful, for then they believe their anger is an inseparable part of who they are, and they stop trusting themselves.

What Makes Anger Arise?

The deepest cause of anger is our ignorance misconceiving reality. In addition to this, other factors contribute to our becoming angry at any particular moment. These include the seed of anger in our mindstream, our habit of getting angry, the inappropriate attention that projects negativity, the strength of our attachment, and contact with external factors. By understanding these causes and conditions for anger to arise, we can then begin to change them and thus tame our anger.

Just as an apple seed needs other conditions, such as water, sunshine, and fertilizer, before it can grow into a tree, the seed of anger is nourished by other factors, such as our previous conditioning or habits, inappropriate attention, and objects we find unpleasant. Thus, in the Buddhist view, anger does not arise from one factor alone, such as a negative childhood experience, but from a complex of factors, beginning with our ignorance which misconceives reality and including other cooperative causes from the past and present. A single traumatic event in our life may have made the seed of anger more easily activated, but it is not entirely responsible for it. As will be seen in the following chapters, even this rudimentary understanding of dependent arising—in this case how anger arises dependent on many factors—can interrupt our habit of trying to find "the cause" to blame, and therefore can help to diffuse our anger.

The Seed of Anger

From a Buddhist viewpoint, anger is not always present in our mind. We have many emotions, attitudes, cognitions, and so forth, all arising and falling away. When the mental factor of anger is manifest in our mind, we are angry. When that anger subsides, the seed of anger still remains in our mindstream, but this is the potential of anger, not the mental factor of anger, not a state of mind or a consciousness. Thus, while the potential exists to get angry in the future, we may not be actively angry at present.

The seed of anger is to be distinguished from a low-grade hostility that may affect many aspects of our life. The latter is a small degree of manifest anger that we fail to identify because our introspective alertness is not highly developed. As with all anger, it does not permeate everything we do. It is manifest sometimes and in seed form other times. As we meditate and are able to identify our mental factors more quickly and easily, we will consciously recognize the presence of low-grade anger that was previously unobserved. This gives us a great advantage in dealing with it.

From a Buddhist viewpoint, the seed of anger has been with us since birth—and even before, since we accept past lives. Anger and its seed are not the nature of our mind. They are like clouds that obscure the open spaciousness of the sky. Anger is based on the ignorance misconceiving the nature of reality. When we generate the wisdom understanding the nature of reality, we are able to gradually erase anger and its seed from our mental continuum so that they can never arise again. Eliminating all destructive emotions and disturbing attitudes in this way is the purpose of Buddhist practice.

The Habit of Anger

We are all familiar with the power of habit and the difficulty of breaking a bad habit. In addition to ordinary habits, such as taking the same route to work every day, we also have emotional habits. Some people have a strong habit of becoming angry. Their energy easily goes in that direction because in the past they have not cultivated patience by applying the antidotes to anger.

To begin to counteract our habits of resentment, frustration, and so forth, it is helpful to look inside and observe our emotional patterns. Are there particular topics that inevitably provoke agitation in us? Do we habitually feel angry in certain types of situations? Noticing these reactions, we can do further research and ascertain exactly what our mind is projecting and fearing. Then we can re-balance our view, making it more realistic.

We may also be habituated to expressing our anger in particular ways that often make the situation worse. For example, Janet becomes frustrated when her plans don't turn out the way she would like and vents her anger by complaining to family and friends. The more habituated she is to grumbling, the more she feeds her own dissatisfaction. Timothy habitually vents his anger by playing video games, taking his hostility out on the fictitious characters on the screen. This, however, simply familiarizes his mind with anger and deepens his habit of acting out aggressively. The real problems come, of course, when he is so blinded by rage that he ceases to discriminate between fictitious and real people, and his habit simply takes over.

Some of our emotional habits were formed when, as children, we observed and imitated our parents' reactions to events. In addition, our family, culture, and society conditioned us to think and feel in particular ways. Becoming aware of our past conditioning and the habits it formed inside us gives us the opportunity now as adults to re-condition ourselves when necessary. For example, Henry's family members were indignant every time their ethnic group was slurred. He, therefore, was conditioned to think that this was an appropriate emotional reaction and became habituated to it. As an adult, he came to realize that he didn't need to be angry in order to oppose discrimination. By re-framing challenging situations and generating compassion for others who were ignorantly prejudiced, he was able to remain calm, yet speak clearly and forcefully in difficult circumstances.

Inappropriate Attention

As mentioned previously, inappropriate attention is a mental factor that exaggerates certain aspects of people, ideas, situations, and objects, thus creating incorrect stories about them. When we find ourselves ruminating on a problem—attributing negative motivations to someone, convincing ourselves of her ill will, and jumping to conclusions about the dire results of her actions—our inappropriate attention has taken over. While most of us do not consider ourselves capable of writing screenplays, when we look closely at what goes on in our minds, we find that we write melodramas all the time. These soap operas, with ourselves as the stars, ensure we have a steady flow of problems to worry about. This is one job from which we need to resign!

We often assume that everyone who experiences abuse or trauma reacts similarly. However, a friend who, together with her sister, experienced severe abuse as a child commented to me about the difference in their reactions. "For years I harbored rage, while my sister did not. This is probably due to our different habits of anger from past lives and the differing ways our attention related to the abuse in this life." Tibetan refugees frequently do not suffer the same post-traumatic stress as other refugees who have been beaten, tortured, and imprisoned. His Holiness the Dalai Lama attributes this to the fact that the Tibetans' paradigm includes many of the perspectives explained in the following chapters. Working with anger by changing the viewpoint from which we describe a situation to ourselves transforms our inappropriate attention to appropriate attention and has salubrious effects on our mind and relationships.

The Relationship between Attachment and Anger

While anger is fueled by inappropriate attention exaggerating or projecting negative qualities, attachment is fueled by inappropriate attention exaggerating or projecting positive qualities. Attachment is often among the factors giving rise to anger, for the more attached we are to something or someone, the angrier we are when we are denied that. For example, Susan places great value on money as the measure of her success in life. She works hard to accumulate it and feels satisfaction when she does. However, when her stocks went down, she became upset and irate. Similarly, Wayne treasures his new car, so when he found it dented in the parking lot outside his office, he flew into a rage. Jane desperately wanted the promotion at work, and her colleague's getting it filled her with jealousy and resentment.

When we look at our own lives, we will find many similar examples of attachment precipitating anger when we cannot obtain the object of our attachment or are separated from it. As our expectations become increasingly unrealistic, we become increasingly prone to disappointment and anger.

Attachment also gives rise to hurt and fear which, in turn, often underlie anger. For example, when we are attached to a person, we feel hurt when he or she doesn't reciprocate our affection. In an attempt to overcome the feeling of powerlessness we have when we are hurt, we often become angry at the other person. In another case, when we get the dream job we crave, we may become fearful of a colleague usurping it. Unable to admit our fear, we become angry and jealous of the colleague. Here, too, anger can be traced back to attachment.

When attached to an object, we imbue it with more worth than it actually has. Then, we cling to it, thinking we must have it in order to be happy. The "object" of our attachment may be a material possession, place, person, goal, or idea. We may also be attached to being right, being good, or doing things in a certain way, as well as to reputation, image, approval, rules, religious doctrine, political beliefs, and so forth. In all these cases, we project value onto objects that far exceeds their actual worth.

Not all cases of wanting or being positively disposed towards something are attachment. With a balanced attitude, we may aspire to develop love, compassion, wisdom, and patience, and we may seek a spiritual mentor, liberation, and enlightenment. Such virtuous aspirations are founded on accurate understanding and seek happiness from internal mental development.

In contrast, anger and attachment are based on inaccurate projections and operate on the assumption that happiness and suffering come from external sources—objects and people who, by their nature, are transient and cannot provide the lasting peace and happiness we seek. Contemplating the impermanent nature of the person or thing to which we are attached helps us to release the disappointment, hurt, fear, and anger that attachment causes. Thinking deeply about our potential as human beings and our long-term priorities also enables us to focus on what is positive in our life and leave aside these painful emotions.

Contact with External Factors

Contact with particular external factors may also contribute to our becoming angry. Among those mentioned in Buddhist texts are "objects" which appear unpleasant, ill-chosen friends, and certain verbal and written stimuli.

In our lives we inevitably encounter "objects" that appear unpleasant or aggravating. These may be persons, ideas, conditions (such as illness), or situations. When we are first training in patience, avoiding contact with these is advisable. This is done not to escape them, but to give ourselves some mental space to apply the antidotes to anger successfully in our meditation practice or reflection time. With some firm practice under our belt, we can again contact these "objects" and relate to them in a new way.

Avoiding people at whom we tend to get angry is not always possible. In this case, we have to do the best we can. If we feel ourselves becoming agitated around a person, we can leave the situation, telling her that we will get back to her later, when we have calmed down. In this way, we avoid saying or doing things that exacerbate the situation and that we will regret later.

We also need to select our friends carefully. Ill-chosen ones can be detrimental influences and provoke our anger. Upset with a colleague, Peter spoke about it with his friend Terry, who responded, "That person is a jerk. You have to show him who's right and not let him get away with this. Tell everyone in your office what's going on!" Hearing this, Peter's anger flared higher, and the two of them set out devising a plan to humiliate the colleague. Although Terry was supposed to be a friend, in fact he re-enforced Peter's anger, and by encouraging Peter to talk behind his colleague's back, he got everyone in the office stirred up.

We need to choose friends who help us process our anger in a constructive way. When we talk with these friends about a disturbing event, we should not expect them to side with us against the other person. If we do, our words become divisive, so that we are using a harmful form of speech. Instead, recognizing that our anger is our own problem, we should say, "I'm upset and would like your help in working with my anger." This is quite different from saying, "This person made me mad; what should I do?" In the first case, our aim is to subdue our own disturbing emotion. Later, when our mind is calmer, we'll reflect on an appropriate course of action. In the second case, our aim is to fix the external situation without first working with our mind or acknowledging our role in the conflict. Working with our mind first is more important than diving in and blindly trying to fix a problem with an uncontrolled mind.

Verbal, written, and visual stimuli, such as books, magazines, television, the Internet, and radio may also activate our anger. Studies show that to keep the audience's interest, films and programs must create frequent tension points. If we observe our reactions while viewing some films and listening to some music, we will often see our anger arising towards particular characters and events. This re-enforces our judgmental mind and anger.

Recently, one of the prisoners with whom I correspond wrote, "The entertainment media feeds us such a constant stream of violence that we become comfortable with it until, of course, we don't agree with the choice of victim, and then we say it's a crime. The media repeatedly reinforces the use of deadly force to resolve disagreements. How can we honestly be surprised when the children who see this later exhibit violent behavior?" Although television is a popular way for inmates to pass time, this one no longer watches these shows. Instead he studies Buddhist books and does various meditation practices. The change in him has been remarkable.

The great Buddhist masters recommend contemplating these factors that stimulate anger. Becoming aware of the causes and conditions of our anger by examining our own angry reactions is beneficial. This awareness will enable us to work with these causes and conditions constructively. By diminishing them, we will not experience the resultant anger with the same frequency or intensity, and our interactions with the world around us will improve.

Chapter Six

TRAINING IN PATIENCE

The Buddha described a variety of techniques for working with anger by developing patience. Many of these are found in *A Guide to the Bodhisattva's Way of Life* by the great Indian sage Shantideva, as well as in the *lojong*, or thought transformation, teachings of Tibetan Buddhism. The following chapters will detail some of these techniques.

The general strategy for working with anger is first to learn and correctly understand the techniques, which often involve reframing a situation so that we view it from a new perspective. Then we begin to practice these techniques in the peaceful environment of a meditation session or reflection time. This familiarizes our mind with and increases our confidence in a repertoire of alternative ways to look at situations that used to make us angry.

Training ourselves in these techniques when we are not upset or in a tense situation is important. Just as we drive around an empty parking lot in drivers' training to get used to the accelerator, brakes, and steering wheel before going on the highway, so we begin practicing patience in a tranquil environment, not a conflict situation. While sitting quietly, we first remember a situation in which we exploded in anger or an event that brings back feelings of hurt or hostility. Then we apply the techniques to it. For example, we might rerun a mental video of the event, but practice thinking differently within it. By viewing the situation from a new perspective in our meditation, we can decrease our anger and then envision ourselves responding to other people differently. This kind of practice not only helps us dissolve past hurt and grudges, it also familiarizes us with techniques that we can apply in similar situations in the future.

One key to applying the various techniques is to focus on our mental attitude and emotions, not on what to say or do. In our American "fix-it" culture, when we have a conflict, it is all too easy to think, "What should I *do?*" We instantly want to fix the problem by changing factors in the external situation. This tendency comes from the ingrained view that the problem exists "outside," independent of us. However, as discussed before, since the problem begins with the way our mind interprets and reacts to the situation, the solution begins inside our mind as well. Therefore, instead of going around in circles trying to decide what to do, for the time being, we should shelve the urgency to fix the problem and focus on transforming our emotions and attitudes. Once that is done, what to say or do is not so difficult to decide.

The Role of Meditation

As said, to be sufficiently skilled to apply the techniques for subduing anger in our daily life, we must first familiarize ourselves with them during times of quiet meditation. However, although the word "meditation" is used, we do not need to sit with legs crossed and closed eyes to familiarize ourselves with the techniques in this book. We can simply lean back in a comfortable chair and reflect. The Buddha taught a variety of types of meditations that subdue anger and cultivate patience, for example, observing the anger, re-framing the situation, cultivating opposite emotions such as love and compassion, and generating wisdom realizing reality.

The meditation of observing our anger involves sitting quietly and instead of paying attention to the storyline behind the anger, simply noting the various physical and mental sensations that arise and pass as the anger flows through us. We may observe physical sensations such as blood rushing to our head, our heart pounding, or a deadening ache in our stomach. We may note the emotional pain of hurt feelings, disappointment, and unfulfilled expectations. Simply observing these, but not reacting to them by clinging to them or pushing them away, we experience them as they are in the present. In doing so, we watch them arise and cease of their own accord.

A hospice nurse one commented to me that she has noticed that even if people try, they cannot sustain a negative emotion for very long. Whatever grief, anger, despair, or resentment may arise in the mind, its nature is impermanent and it will pass. If we observe closely, we can even note our emotions and thoughts changing moment by moment. Such mindfulness can be very effective in letting go of negative emotions.

Techniques in which we re-frame the situation constitute most of this volume. They fall in the category of analytical meditation, in which we investigate our thoughts, feelings, and perceptions to discern if they are accurate and beneficial. We also practice looking at situations in different ways. Changing the way we describe and interpret situations subdues anger because we stop exaggerating and projecting negativities onto people, situations, and objects. In this way, the external event, its meaning, and our position in it appear to us differently, and our anger evaporates.

Meditations on love and compassion strengthen these positive emotions in our minds and hearts, which is benificial because these emotions act not only as antidotes to anger, but also as measures preventing it from arising. The wisdom realizing reality cuts the ignorance that lies behind anger. This wisdom is generated through a specific type of analytical meditation, as explained later.

Each person will find affinity with certain techniques for working with anger. For some, mindfully observing their emotions and thoughts allows these to subside naturally. For others, a more analytical approach is necessary. Through investigation, they need to see clearly that anger is a distorted state of mind that misapprehends its object. Or they may need to reflect on the disadvantages of anger in order to awaken their determination to step back and not blindly indulge it. Because different approaches work for different people, the Buddha, a skillful teacher, taught a variety of techniques so that each person could establish a repertoire that works well for her.

Don't Expect Anger to Disappear Overnight

Sometimes dissolving our anger even when we are in a peaceful environment is difficult, because we have become locked into our past emotions and misconceptions. But if we keep trying, we will gradually subdue it. Then, when we go to work, school, or family gatherings, we will have at least a "fighting chance" to work with our anger should it arise. With constant practice over time, we will be able to prevent anger from manifesting. As we develop the wisdom realizing the emptiness of inherent existence (explained in Chapter Eighteen) and actualize higher stages of the path, we will be able to eliminate anger and its seed from our mindstream completely.

Elizabeth's practice is a good illustration of this gradual progression. Like many people, she was sensitive to criticism and at the slightest hint of it would become angry, either lashing out at the other person or withdrawing and sulking. After hearing teachings on patience, she discussed them with friends who had also heard them and asked her teacher questions to make sure she understood the teachings correctly. Then, in her meditation, she recalled past situations in which she had been criticized that were still emotionally charged for her. She practiced the various techniques involving new ways of looking at what had happened. For example, sometimes she looked at her own hypersensitivity and tried to let go of the preconceptions underlying it. At first, her mind was resistant, always saying, "Yes, but..." and then thinking of more reasons why she was right and the other person was wrong. After being criticized, she would still find herself talking behind the other's back to retaliate. But when she got home at night, she would sit quietly and apply the techniques until the anger diminished. She did purification practices, which involved regretting her behavior and resolving to avoid it in the future, and the next day, she tried to rectify the situation with the other person.

She continued her practice, and slowly the new ways of framing the situations became more familiar and comfortable in her mind. In her daily life, she could not think of the antidotes fast enough in actual situations and would still flare up inside. But when she recognized anger arising, she was able to stop verbally retaliating and creating a scene. As she practiced more, the antidotes became more familiar, and she could recall and apply them at the actual time the criticism was being received. Now, when a situation ended, her heart was calm and she no longer carried animosity around with her the rest of the day. Patience, love, compassion, and altruism were more firm in her mind now. Needless to say, her relationships with others improved dramatically, as did her internal sense of well-being.

As Elizabeth's meditation practice develops over the years (and life times!), she will gain single-pointed concentration, and thus the manifest destructive emotions will not arise in her mind for long stretches of time. She will continue studying the Dharma (the Buddha's teachings, the path to enlightenment), contemplating it, and meditating on it until she realizes emptiness directly. Then she will use this wisdom to cleanse anger and its seed from her mindstream completely.

Subduing anger is a slow and steady process. Don't expect it to disappear overnight. Reacting in anger is a deeply ingrained habit, and like all bad habits, it takes time to unlearn. Developing patience requires a great deal of effort—and patience!

Let's now begin looking at some techniques—often called "antidotes" because they neutralize the poison of negative emotions, in this case anger.

Understand Each Other's Needs and Concerns

Two parties in conflict often talk past each other. Each one is certain that what he thinks the main issue is, the motivation he has attributed to the other person, and the way the situation appears to him are accurate. However, often these interpretations are flawed. A few examples will clarify this point.

At age seventeen, Sarah was sure her parents were over-protective. They always wanted to know exactly where she was, whom she was with, and what time she would be home. If she was going to be even ten minutes late, she had to phone her parents so they wouldn't worry that she had been in a car accident. Her parents, on the other hand, loved Sarah and wanted to make sure she was safe. They were concerned that she may not yet be able to assess and handle potentially difficult situations. Sarah and her parents fought regularly over this, making all of their lives unpleasant. The more Sarah tried to assert that she was capable of making decisions, the more her parents seemed to try to restrict her movements, and the more her parents did that, the more she asserted herself. They were caught in a vicious circle.

Several years later Sarah encountered the Dharma and began to meditate. When the situation with her parents kept distracting her during her meditation, she knew she had to look at it more closely. In doing so, Sarah saw that she and her parents were talking past each other and quarreling over two different issues. For her, the conflict was about autonomy and independence. She felt like she was an adult and knew how to make wise decisions. She resented what she perceived to be her parents' lack of trust, their interference in her life, and their trying to control her. She then realized that for her parents, the conflict was about safety. Looking at the situation from their viewpoint, she began to see that her parents were not trying to control her life. Rather, because they loved her, they wanted her to be safe. Once she saw this, Sarah was able to let go of her resentment and stop quarreling with her parents. Once one partner in an argument has resigned, the argument can no longer occur, so her parents also relaxed.

In this instance, it was Sarah who realized that the needs and concerns of the conflicting parties were different. It could equally have been her parents. Had they realized that their daughter had tools to make decisions and was not simply being brash and rebellious, they would have spoken to their teenager with more respect, which would have elicited a different response from her.

Although Sarah's parents, from time to time, still seemed overly concerned about her, Sarah stopped being annoyed. An incident between her grandmother and her father confirmed her understanding of her parents' concerns and the foolishness of becoming angry at them. One day, when her father was sixty-five, his mother reminded him to put on a sweater before he went out so he didn't catch cold. Sarah chuckled at this and realized that her parents would probably check on her in a similar way her whole life, no matter how old she was.

Years later, when Sarah was in her thirties, her mother asked her to wear a certain dress to the family Christmas party that evening. Sarah happily complied. Her cousin, who had overheard the conversation, later said to her, "I was aghast that your mother told you what to wear when you're thirty-five, and I'm even more surprised that you didn't explode at her for doing so." Sarah explained to her cousin, "Unlike when I was a teenager, I'm now confident of myself as an independent adult. My mother's saying that doesn't threaten my confidence or my autonomy. In fact, now I'm happy to do something small to please her, for she and my dad cared for me with so much love when I was young."

Due to misunderstanding each other's needs and concerns, miscommunication occurs on the international level as well. During the Gulf War, I was in Malaysia, which is a predominantly Muslim country. There I heard the BBC news and read the English-language paper published in Kuala Lumpur. After the war, I returned to the USA and at my parents' house watched the news reviewing the war. They seemed to be discussing two different wars. From the American viewpoint, the war was about one matter and from the viewpoint of many Islamic nations, it was about another. I had a similar experience visiting the Gaza Strip in the late 1990s. The Palestinians there had one view of Arafat as a negotiator and the Americans had a different one.

In all these situations—personal and international—freeing ourselves from our narrow understanding of a situation by seeing it from the other's viewpoint is an effective remedy for anger. We can ask ourselves, "If I had grown up in that person's family, society, time in history, and cultural conditions, what would my needs and concerns be in this situation?"

When we look at the situation from the other person's viewpoint, sometimes we see that she perceives it differently than we thought she did. Other times, we realize that we have little idea of how a situation appears to another person or what her needs and concerns are. Therefore, we need to ask her; and when she responds, we need to *listen,* without interrupting. It is all too easy, when someone explains her view to us, to correct her or tell her that she should not feel the way she does. This only inflames the other person, and convinces her, with good reason, that we don't understand. Rather, we need to listen from our heart to what she says. After she has fully expressed herself, we can share our perspectives, and generally, a productive discussion will ensue.

Ask Ourselves Whether the Other Person Is Happy

Another technique for working with anger is to ask ourselves, "Is the person who is harming me happy?" Suppose someone shouts at us and complains about almost everything we do. Is he happy or miserable? Obviously, he's miserable. That's why he's acting this way. If he were happy, he wouldn't be quarrelsome.

We all know what it's like to be unhappy, and that is exactly how the other person feels right now. Let's stop seeing the situation from our self-centered perspective and put ourselves in his shoes. When we're unhappy and "letting it all out," how would we like others to react? Generally, we want them to understand and help us. That is exactly how the other person feels. Given that he is unhappy and would like help, how can we be angry with him? He should be the object of our compassion, not our anger. If we think like this, we'll find our hearts filled with patience and loving-kindness for the other, no matter how he acts toward us. In fact, we may even feel inspired to help him.

How can we help someone who is angry at us? Each situation is different and must be examined individually. However, some general guidelines may apply. First, we can pause, listen, and consider whether the other's complaints about us are justified. If so, we can apologize and correct the situation. That often stops his anger. Second, when people are upset and angry, we can try to be calm and not argue back, because in their present state of mind, they won't be able to listen to us. This is understandable, because we, too, don't listen to others when we're angry. So, it's better to help them settle down and talk about the situation later.

When we discuss disagreements, engaging in reflective, or active, listening is helpful. Here, we summarize our understanding of how the situation appears in the other's eyes and her feelings, needs, and concerns, without commenting on any of these. This allows us to check whether our interpretations of what she is thinking and feeling are accurate, and it also lets her know that we have understood her feelings, needs, and concerns. She will relax when she feels that we understand what she is saying. Then, we tell her how the situation appears to us and our feelings, needs, and concerns. Dialogue can now ensue.

Chapter Seven

COPING WITH CRITICISM

> Since ancient times it has been the case
> That those who speak too much are criticized,
> As are those who speak too little
> And those who don't speak at all.
> Everyone in this world is criticized.
> —*The Dhammapada*

Receiving criticism is an unpleasant and all too frequent experience. While we work hard to obtain some things—money, love, and so forth—criticism comes without our asking for it! When it does, our knee-jerk reaction is usually hurt and anger. We may turn that anger inward, doubting and blaming ourselves, or we may turn it outwards and criticize the other person or ruin her good reputation by talking behind her back.

When we receive criticism, we usually feel that we're the only person that is so obviously mistreated: "I'm doing my best, but the boss always overlooks others' mistakes and inevitably notices mine. Everybody's always getting on my case!" However, when we check with other people, we find that almost everyone feels he is criticized unfairly or too much. Unfortunately, we have to admit that, because we are self-centered, the injustice and pain of the criticism we receive seem greater than everyone else's. When we put our situation into perspective and realize that at one time or another everyone is unjustly blamed (or justly held responsible!), distress over our own situation diminishes. For example, I was fuming over a comment which unfairly blamed me for something I had not done. Then suddenly the thought entered my mind, "Millions of people get criticized every day. This is not an uncommon experience. In addition, this isn't the first time someone has blamed me unjustly and it won't be the last. I'd better get used to this, because unsatisfactory experiences are the nature of cyclic existence." Before I knew it, the tension and anger had evaporated.

When someone criticizes us, our instant reaction is generally anger. What prompts this response? Our conception of the situation. Although we may not be consciously aware of it, one part of our mind holds the view "I'm a great person. If I slip up and make a mistake, it's a small one. This person has completely misunderstood the situation. He's making a big deal out of my little mistake and declaring it at the top of his voice to the whole world! He's wrong!" This description is oversimplified, but if we are honest with ourselves, we will recognize that we do think in this way. Are these conceptions correct? Are we perfect or nearly so? Obviously not.

Acknowledge Our Mistakes

Consider a situation in which we make a mistake and someone notices it. If that person were to come along and tell us we have a nose on our face, would we be angry? No. Why not? Because our nose is obvious. It's there for the world to see. Someone merely saw it and commented upon it. Our faults and mistakes are similar. They're obvious, and people see them. A person noticing them is merely commenting on what is evident to everyone. Why should we get angry? If we aren't upset when someone says we have a nose, why should we be when he tells us we have faults?

We would be more relaxed if we acknowledged, "Yes, you're right. I made a mistake," or "Yes, I have a bad habit." Instead of putting on a show of "I'm perfect, so how dare you say that!" we could just admit our error and apologize. Having faults means we're normal, not hopeless. Frequently, acknowledging our error and apologizing diffuses the situation.

It's so hard for us to say, "I'm sorry," isn't it? Our pride often prevents us from admitting our mistakes, even though both we and the other person know we made them. We feel we'll lose face by apologizing, or we'll become less important or worthwhile. We fear the other person will have power over us if we admit our mistake. In order to defend ourselves, we then attack back, diverting the attention from ourselves to the other. This strategy—which does not resolve the conflict—is commonly practiced on kindergarten playgrounds, as well as in national and international politics.

Contrary to our fearful misconceptions, apologizing indicates inner strength, not weakness. We have enough honesty and self-confidence that we don't pretend to be faultless. We can admit our mistakes. So many tense situations can be diffused by the simple words "I'm sorry." Often all the other person wants is for us to acknowledge his or her pain and our role in it.

Learn from Our Critics

When others criticize us, we should consider whether there is truth in what they say. Disregarding their tone of voice and choice of words, we can think about the content of their words. If it contains some truth, then these people are in fact helping us to improve. We often say, "I want to improve. I want to eliminate my weakness and become a kinder person." Yet, when people offer advice—especially if it is with a loud or sarcastic tone of voice—we don't want to hear! We cry, "Hold on! You can tell me how to improve only when I want to hear it, only with a kind attitude and pleasant voice, and only if I can handle it at the moment." That's a lot to expect from others! Since we cannot control when, what, why, and how they give us negative feedback, we would benefit from strengthening our own abilities to process it constructively. We can do this by concentrating on the relevant content of what they say and using it to improve ourselves. Then we can thank them sincerely for their comments, no matter how they were expressed.

In fact, excellent practitioners even seek out criticism. For this reason, Togme Sangpo in *The Thirty-seven Practices of Bodhisattvas* says:

> Though someone may deride and speak bad words
> About you in a public gathering,
> Looking on him as a spiritual teacher,
> Bow to him with respect—
> This is the practice of bodhisattvas.

In other words, when we are sincerely focused on improving our-selves, we consider those who point out our faults as teachers guiding us in our chosen direction. Even if they criticize us unjustly, we see them as pointing out how unnecessarily defensive we become when falsely accused.

Deal with False Criticism Calmly

Let's suppose we're criticized for something we didn't do or are ac-cused of making a huge mistake when we made only a small one. Still, there's no reason to get angry. This is like somebody telling us we have antlers on our head. We know we don't have them. The person who says that is clearly mistaken. Similarly, if someone blames us unjustly, there's no reason to become angry or depressed, because what she says is incorrect.

Of course this does not mean we should passively accept someone's incorrect speech without attempting to rectify the misun-derstanding. Using our discriminating wisdom, we need to examine each situation individually. Sometimes it's better just to let the remark go and not try to correct it, even later. If it's a trivial matter, the other person may later realize her mistake. Even if she doesn't, trying to explain what happened may only start a bigger argument. For ex-ample, if our roommate is in a bad mood and mistakenly blames us for leaving in the sink plates that are actually his dirty dishes, letting his false accusation go may be wiser. If we try to explain our viewpoint when he is already irritable, he may become even angrier. Similarly, correcting everyone every time he or she said anything inaccurate would be a nuisance. No one would like having us around!

When we decide not to respond to a critical remark, we must observe our mind to see if we have genuinely let go. If we have, no further build up of resentment will occur. If we haven't, a certain edginess will still exist in our mind. Sooner or later, our indignation will reach critical mass and we will explode. Genuine letting go means that we have dealt with our anger and our heart is peaceful.

Communicate Well

In other situations, we need to explain our actions and the evolution of the misunderstanding to the other person, even if it is painful. For example, when our behavior hurts a close friend, we need to explain our action and motivation and do our best to assuage his anger. However, discussing such misunderstandings and disagreements is better left until neither we nor the other is in the heat of anger. Trying to do otherwise may only make the situation worse, since we don't express ourselves well when we're angry. Thus, we first need to excuse ourselves from the situation and calm our mind, ideally by practicing some of the techniques for pacifying anger. If the other person is angry, we need to give him some space and approach him later when his mind is more open. Later, when we do explain our actions and the evolution of the misunderstanding to the other person, speaking gently, not antagonistically, is more effective. We lose nothing by being humble and offering an honest explanation.

Sometimes pride blocks us from talking honestly with another person about sore points between us. We may want to ignore him or dismiss him by saying, "Your anger is your problem." Such behavior is arrogant and cruel and arises from hurt and fear. We need to stop and ask ourselves, "What is going on inside me? How can I open my heart to acknowledge my own pain as well as the pain of this other person?" In such situations, our hearts will open if we remember that both we and the other equally want to be happy and avoid suffering. Then, we can wish happiness and freedom from misery for both of us.

Perhaps no overt disagreement has occurred, yet we are uncomfortable with another person's seemingly critical remarks or hostile body language. Such events naturally arise when we share an environment and resources with others. We need to communicate with others and perhaps give them feedback that may not be pleasing to their ears. But to be truly effective, we must do this with a motivation of kindness, not anger. Although sometimes our exploding in anger may wake up the other person and inspire discussion, it may also make the situation worse or prevent communication. Thus it's best if we can first use one of the techniques described here to subdue our hostility and then approach the other person and explain to him how the situation appears to us and how we feel, without blaming him for our feelings. We can share our interests and concerns, listen to his, and try to find a solution that benefits all parties as much as possible.

Leave the Situation if Necessary

Sometimes finding a satisfactory resolution is difficult. A person once said to His Holiness the Dalai Lama, "Someone at my office is often verbally abusive. I've tried to practice patience, and I've also tried to discuss the situation with the person, but my anger remains and the situation is too stressful for me. What should I do?" His Holiness responded, "If you feel the situation is more than you can handle right now, change jobs!"

Learn to Evaluate Ourselves

One reason others' criticism affects us so deeply is that we are afraid that it may be true. This occurs because we have never learned to evaluate our actions. Since childhood, we have relied on others to tell us if what we do is good or bad. As children we needed to do this, but now as adults, we need to develop the ability to evaluate our own actions. Otherwise, if we simply rely on others to tell us who we are, we will become very confused because their opinions differ.

This became clear to me one morning years ago while I was director of a monastery. A nun came to see me and complained, "You are so uptight and strict about the way you keep your vows. I wish you'd relax a little bit." A few minutes after she had left, another nun came in and said, "You are so loose in the way you keep your vows. It's a horrible example for others. You need to be stricter." All I could do was laugh inside at the absurdity of it all. If I had depended on others to tell me who I was, I would have been lost, for they had opposite views!

We have all had the experience of being praised for an action, but still not feeling good inside about it. Why not? Generally, although the action looked admirable from the outside, our motivation was selfish or egotistical. We know the reality of our internal motivation, and we have to live with ourselves. All the praise in the world cannot remedy that.

Similarly, we may have had the experience of acting with a well-thought-out and positive motivation, but receiving criticism for our action. If we are confident in the purity of our motivation and did the best we could in the situation, there is no reason to doubt ourselves afterwards.

Thus, being aware of our motivation as much as possible and deliberately cultivating a positive one are essential to our peace of mind. By doing this, we will avoid acting destructively, and if we do because we neglect to check our motivation, we will be able to acknowledge and correct our mistake. Similarly, should others misunderstand our actions, we will be free of self-doubt and remain steadfast. Learning to evaluate and correct our motivation and actions requires time and effort spent in introspection, and it is well worthwhile.

Allow Others Their Opinions

What do we do when people criticize our religious or political beliefs? We know that others are entitled to their own opinions, even if they disagree with ours, but one part of our mind may say, "Everyone has to agree with my ideas!" If that part of our mind is especially active and defensive, we need to ask, "What inside me feels insecure about others' not sharing my beliefs?" Then we need to listen openly to ourselves, and if we are thinking in a confused way, we need to guide ourselves back to a reasonable outlook.

We may falsely equate others not agreeing with our beliefs with their criticizing them. This is not necessarily the case, for many people are tolerant of those with differing views. Having different opinions does not imply conflict and quarrels. Thus, it is incorrect to assume that others disapprove or are antagonistic towards us because our ideas do not coincide with theirs.

Jill, a Buddhist practitioner, became defensive when her uncle commented that she was practicing a "strange, Eastern religion." Then she recalled that others' criticism cannot hurt the Buddha, Dharma, or Sangha. The path to enlightenment exists whether others recognize it as such or not. She saw that her agitation stemmed from attachment to her beliefs. Because her ego was involved, she felt compelled to prove her beliefs were right. Relaxing, she knew she didn't need others' approval to practice her faith. She had examined the Buddha's teachings well and was thus secure in her belief, so why should her uncle's criticism disturb her peace of mind? His criticism didn't mean her beliefs were wrong, nor did it mean she was stupid or bad. He simply had another opinion, that's all.

Sometimes we can give others information and correct their misconceptions, but sometimes people are closed-minded and find it difficult to listen to views different from their own. There's nothing we can do then, except maintain a kind attitude towards them.

Don't See Criticism Where There Is None

We have already discussed our mind's tendency to engage in the creative writing of screenplays starring Me. One way this manifests is by our fabricating criticism where there is none. For example, Betsy had just had a baby and was flying to Vermont to see her sister for the first time since the birth. She said to me, "I'm sure the moment I step off the plane, my sister will take one look at me and say, 'Hmm, you've put on weight!' I can't stand the idea of her doing that!" I tried to explain that she looked fine and that pregnant mothers are supposed to gain weight. Betsy wouldn't hear any of it, and I sadly thought, "Even if her sister says sincerely, 'You look great,' Betsy will think that she's ridiculing her!"

Our mind is good at projecting ill treatment. One evening as I was leaving the meditation hall, Susan approached me and said, "The flowers on the altar are the nuns' responsibility. They are untidy right now, and I'm sure our teacher is unhappy about this." Her comment took me by surprise, and although I said nothing, inside my resentful mind was saying, "Wait a minute! Who said the flowers are the nuns' responsibility? I never heard that! Anyway, they look fine. And even if they didn't, our teacher wouldn't complain about them." We walked on a few steps. She was saying something, but by that time my internal defense system was cranked up. "She's guilt tripping me! The flowers are no more my responsibility than hers. People in this organization often say underhanded things like that, pretending to make an innocent comment but actually running a guilt trip. This has happened to me so many times in the past!" And I began to recall several such instances. While I had been tired upon leaving the meditation hall, I was now wide awake. Although we parted ways at the intersection of two paths, my anger kept going.

But it was late at night and I didn't want to lose precious sleep, so I laid my anger aside, vowing to return to it the next day. After all, I wasn't really angry. I was right! However, the next morning when I was all set to rev up my defenses, it occurred to me that the guilt trip was not coming from the side of her words. Rather, my mind was imputing a particular meaning to her remarks. Seeing this clearly, I found the anger had faded and died, just like the flowers probably had by that time.

Our tendency to project criticism where there is none comes from unproductive emotional habits. It also is a karmic result of criticizing and judging others in the past. When our mind is well accustomed to find faults with others, we incorrectly assume they will do the same with us. Here we have two useless habits to counteract: the first is judging others, and the second is assuming others are judging us.

Counteract the Critical, Judgmental Attitude

In this chapter, we have discussed how to deal with our anger when others criticize us. We also need to work with our tendency to criticize others. When we observe our mind closely, most of us find that we have opinions about everyone and everything. Even when we are waiting in line at the store, our mind is like a sportscaster with a running commentary on everyone around us. "This person is too loud. That one's too quiet. Why does this person part his hair like that? It's so weird! That woman's clothes don't fit properly. This man's pants are dirty," and on and on. This could actually be humorous if we weren't so involved in believing it all!

This critical, judgmental attitude, which projects negativity on others, is backed by a feeling of discontent. It is also an indirect cause of our anger. First, it prompts us to assume others are criticizing us when they are not. Second, it sours our relationships and induces others to criticize us in return.

Why do we judge others like this? Some misinformed part of our mind thinks that if we criticize others, then we must be superior to them. For this same reason, we get together with friends and gossip about others in the office. Our mind thinks, "If this person and that person are all flawed, well we must be the only wonderful ones!"

However, this way of thinking and relating to others doesn't make us happy. So many people tell me how miserable their judgmental attitude makes them. What to do? Press the stop button on the newscast. In other words, when we realize our mind is preoccupied with the negative and broadcasting unkind remarks, we can just stop. Focus on our breath. Remind ourself that all sentient beings have been kind to us, and that all are just like us in wanting only happiness and not wanting any problems. By readjusting our way of looking at others, we will see them in a different, and kinder, way. And as a result, our anger will decrease.

Chapter Eight

THE BLAMING GAME

See How We Co-create Situations

Another technique to counteract anger is to examine how we became involved in difficult situations. Often we feel we are the innocent victim of unfair people or circumstances. "Poor me! I'm innocent. I didn't do anything, and now this nasty person is taking advantage of me!"

Other people don't make us into a victim. By getting angry, we make ourselves into one. We may be the object of another's anger or abuse, but we needn't be the victim of it. Someone else may blame or harm us, but we become a victim and become trapped in a victim mentality only when we conceive of the situation in a certain way and get angry. The meaning of this is quite profound. Let's look at it in more depth, first using an example of two adults in conflict.

Suppose our partner is upset with our behavior and lashes out at us. We often react by feeling, "I didn't do anything. I'm getting dumped on unfairly." Is this interpretation of the experience accurate? Instead of immediately losing our temper and blaming the other person, let's recognize that the existence of this situation depends on many factors, including both the other person and ourselves.

First, let's look at what we might have done in this life that resulted in our being mistreated. How might we have co-created this situation? Did we do something that aggravated or hurt the other person and made his acting this way toward us more likely? Looking inside, we must be honest with ourselves. Maybe we really weren't so innocent. Maybe we were trying to manipulate the other person and he didn't fall for it. Instead he got upset, and then we acted hurt and offended. But, in fact, our own behavior contributed to the situation.

Some people may be concerned that this is blaming the victim and encouraging people to take responsibility for others' behavior. It isn't. For example, a woman may have done something innocently or intentionally that annoyed her husband, but it isn't her fault if he beats her. His unacceptable and cruel behavior is his responsibility. However, if she can look at the situation from a wide perspective, she may notice that in some instances, her behaviors trigger his. This empowers her to avoid those behaviors and thus to avoid finding herself in similar unpleasant situations in the future. In many instances, the husband may react violently no matter what she does. In these cases, she may recognize that her own emotional attachment and dependency keep her in a harmful situation. This empowers her to counteract them and free herself from an injurious relationship. By acknowledging her misdirected motivations, she will be more aware when forming relationships and, to the best of her ability, will create healthier ones in the future.

Examining the role our behavior played in the evolution of a bad situation doesn't mean blaming ourselves for things that aren't our responsibility and feeling guilty as a result. Getting down on ourselves is actually another trick of the self-centered attitude. It exaggerates our own importance by thinking, "If I'm not the best, then at least I'm the worst."

We generally frame unfortunate or painful circumstances in terms of blame. Either we or the other party is to blame. "Fault" and "blame" are very harsh words in our culture: they imply being evil and guilty. This way of conceiving situations leads to a dead-end. If we blame the other, we become angry, outraged, and vindictive. If we blame ourselves, we become depressed and self-destructive. It's impossible to heal when we're caught up in blaming.

In addition, blaming oversimplifies a complex situation. While every situation arises from a multiplicity of causes and conditions, blaming makes it look like only one cause exists. If we blame the other person, we give him more power than he actually has, for by himself alone, he cannot cause such damage. He can do so only in the context of a situation in which many other people, ourselves included, participate. Similarly, if we blame ourselves, we make ourselves more important than we actually are. People often do this, by saying, for example, "The marriage ended because I wasn't loving enough," or "The project failed because I botched it up." Unfortunately, we have to realize that we aren't so powerful that we can cause everything to go wrong all by ourselves!

Framing situations in terms of blame is both inaccurate and useless. Rather, in each situation, we need to evaluate which factors are our responsibility and which are others' responsibility. This involves clearly reflecting on the situation, without exaggerating either our own or others' power or importance. In this way, we will observe the factors that we contributed, make amends for them, and try to avoid them in the future. We will also discern which factors others contributed, and although we may not condone their actions, we can feel compassion for their confusion.

Such reflection reveals to us the complexity of a situation, for we recognize that the factors contributing to it come from many sources. For example, we want to spend more time with a friend, but she is preoccupied with other affairs. Feeling ignored, we grumble about it. That irritates our friend who then avoids us. In this case, we needn't blame ourselves for complaining or blame our friend for being insensitive. Instead, we can realize that the situation is dependently arising. Some of the causes came from us, some from our friend. Both of us were reacting in habitual patterns rather than discerning what we were feeling and trying to communicate in a kind and accurate way to the other. Recognizing this, we can have compassion for both ourselves and our friend. After becoming clearer about our own feelings, we can initiate discussion about the situation with her.

Look from a Broader Perspective

We can also look at unfortunate events from a broader perspective—in the light of many lifetimes. This involves the topic of karma, or intentional actions. As discussed earlier, from a Buddhist viewpoint, our physical, verbal, and mental actions leave imprints on our consciousness. These imprints later will ripen and influence our experiences. What we experience now is a result of thoughts, feelings, words, and deeds in the past. For example, if someone beats us, we must have done something previously, in this case, physically harmed others. Karma is like a boomerang. We throw it out, and it comes back to us. If we treat others in a certain way, we create specific energy, which then causes something similar to happen to us later.

Understanding this allows us to accept some responsibility for difficult situations. We are not victims; we are co-creators. We reap the results of what we have sown. In the past we have harmed others, even in this life. As children we fought with our playmates on the playground; as adults we have hurt others' feelings. When others then harm us, it's helpful to remember that we're experiencing the results of our previous harmful actions.

We should not be surprised when the imprints of our negative actions ripen. After all, when we plant seeds in the ground, they will grow one day when all the conditions—sunshine, water, and nutrients—are present. Similarly, when we plant detrimental karmic seeds in our mindstream, they will ripen when conducive conditions are present. If we accept this, we'll see there's no reason to blame others for our misfortune. They are just a cooperative condition. We ourselves created the principal cause for our being in any difficult situation.

However, we should not misinterpret this as blaming the victim and vindicating the perpetrator. We should not masochistically blame ourselves, thinking, "I deserve it when people persecute me." For example, Joan believed that because she had abused others in previous lives, her karma had caused her to be reborn into an abusive family where she experienced the suffering she deserved as punishment for her past misdeeds. This misunderstanding of karma prevented her from moving forward into therapy. As she discussed her outlook with her therapist and religious advisor, Joan realized that she was perpetuating her suffering by misusing religious beliefs to blame herself for something she had no control over as a child. As she corrected her view, she was able to continue her process of healing and greatly improve her life.

When we experience problems or suffering, we should acknowledge, "Yes, I harmed others in the past. Now the result is coming back to me. This doesn't mean I'm a bad person. It simply means that under the influence of my own self-centered ignorance, I acted mistakenly and harmed others in the past. If I don't like this experience, then I should be careful how I act towards others so that I don't again create the causes to meet with similar painful situations in the future."

For example, Ken was working on a project with Pat, who constantly seemed to sabotage his good efforts by criticizing him and rousing others to impede his work. At first, Ken felt discouraged and complained about Pat, after which he felt worse and Pat opposed him even more. Finally, Ken stopped, and reflecting on karma and its results, thought, "I must have sabotaged others' efforts in the past, either in this or previous lives." He remembered working on a project with a friend in college and then stealing most of the credit for himself. "If I've acted in such ways in this life, it's quite possible that I did worse in previous lives. In addition, instead of doing purification practices, I've spent a lot of time sitting in front of the TV. It's really no wonder that this problem has come to me. I created the principal cause for this by my own self-centered actions. Pat is simply the cooperative condition." Thinking in this way, he ceased being mad at Pat and decided to encourage people who were doing good work and to cooperate more with others in the future.

By looking at situations in this way, we will learn from our mistakes. Remembering the exact action we did in this or a past life that has brought our present problem is not important. Simply having a general feeling for the kinds of actions we might have done in the past that could precipitate the present occurrence is sufficient. Then we can make a strong determination not to do those actions in the future.

The chapter on karma and its results in any book about *lamrim*, or the gradual path to enlightenment, contains useful information on the workings of karma. It details the ten destructive actions and their results, the ten constructive actions and their results, factors that make an action heavy or light, methods to purify negative imprints, means to protect positive imprints from being damaged, and so on. In addition, a booklet entitled *The Wheel of Sharp Weapons* by Dharmaraksita explains the links between our current experiences and our past actions. It also encourages us to abandon the self-centered attitude and the self-grasping ignorance that spur us to act negatively.

By training ourselves to think in this way, we can transform bad situations into the path to enlightenment by thinking about them in constructive ways. We cease framing situations in terms of blame, fault, and guilt. We examine the evolution of the problem and our responsibility in its co-creation. In this way, we understand what we can do to alter it, and we learn from our experiences rather than get stuck in a victim mentality.

Handle Illness Wisely

We get angry not only at others who seem to interfere with our happiness, but also at illnesses that makes us miserable. Seeing our illness as a manifestation of our past negative karma can help us to let go of self-pity and anger and to transform a painful situation into the path to enlightenment.

A friend of mine on retreat at a monastery in Nepal developed a severe boil on her cheek. Upset at the pain as well as the inconvenience, her mind was looking for someone or something to blame—the person who gave her the virus, the bad living conditions that diminished her immune system, anything. On a walk around the grounds, she encountered our teacher, whom she expected to be sympathetic and to comfort her. Instead, he looked at the boil and exclaimed, "This is great! You're so fortunate!" Then, he explained, "This is a result of destructive actions you've done in the past. It's much better that this karmic imprint ripen now, in this way, than ripen later in longer-lasting or more severe suffering. By experiencing this comparatively minor suffering, the imprint of that action is exhausted and no longer obscures your mindstream." Returning to her room, she thought about it and came to see the situation in this way. She still went to the doctor, but now was in better spirits, the self-pity and resentment having disappeared. Having accepted her situation and stopped fighting the "injustice of it all," she had free attention to notice others and have compassion for them.

Someone may ask, "Does this mean that when we cause people misery, this is a positive karmic action, because we are helping people to purify their negative karma? No, not when our minds are belligerent and vengeful. The technique of considering harm received as purification of negative karma is to be used to help us deal with suffering that we cannot prevent. We must not invert it, rationalizing our own base intentions and harmful behavior. Rather, we should train our minds in compassion.

Chapter Nine

WHEN OUR BUTTONS ARE PUSHED

Know What Our Buttons Are

Each of us has "buttons"—areas where we are sensitive. When our buttons are pushed, we fly off the handle, blaming the other person for upsetting us. But our being upset is a dependently arising process. We contribute the buttons, and the other person does the pushing. If we didn't have the buttons, others couldn't push them.

Our buttons are our responsibility. As long as we have them, someone will push them, especially since they are big, red, and flashing. Our buttons are so sensitive, that even if a person walks by, the breeze from his passage will trigger our button's detector and our alarm will ring, "That person is offending (harming, criticizing, deceiving, manipulating, cheating, etc.) me!" Although many times people have no intention of harming us, our buttons get pushed just because they are so sensitive.

For example, Helen prided herself in being a good mother. She dearly loved her child, was conscientious about her safety, and made sure she had many opportunities to learn and play. Because the preschool was just a few blocks away, she would occasionally ask friends to pick up her daughter when they were passing by. Even if a friend didn't have a car seat, Helen didn't worry, for the drive was so short. One day, when her friend Carleen was coming to visit, Helen asked her to pick up her child on the way. Carleen said, "I can't because I don't have a car seat. We mothers must be informed, and an informed mother knows that a young child *never* rides in a car without a car seat."

Helen interpreted "informed mother" to mean "good mother" and was offended by Carleen's insinuation. She brooded for several days, until she realized that her hypersensitivity was responsible for her mood. She thought, "Carleen and I have different opinions, and that's fine. Not everyone needs to have the same ideas about car seats. I feel that I'm informed, and my decision is reasonable. I know that I care for my child properly. There's no reason for me to take Carleen's remark personally, thinking that a mere difference of opinions means I'm a negligent mother." She let go of her sullenness and felt confident again.

We need to do internal research, asking ourselves what our buttons are and why we are so sensitive in those particular areas. Our sensitivity generally has to do with attachment. In the above example, Helen was attached to approval. If we are able to identify and then reduce our attachments, our buttons shrink. Then even if someone wants to push them, doing so is harder. Realized spiritual beings have no buttons left to push, so no matter how others treat them, they do not become upset.

We may think that if someone deliberately insults us, it's correct to be angry. However, such thinking is illogical. We would be giving our power to the other person, in which case his intention—which we cannot control—would be governing our happiness and suffering. Whether or not another person wishes us ill does not matter. We still have a choice whether to be offended. The less we are attached, for example, to praise and reputation, the less miffed we will become, because our mind will not interpret situations as personal assaults.

Close the Internal Courtroom

When we feel someone has wronged us, we may ruminate on it for hours, days, weeks, and even years, going over the situation again and again in our mind. Inside of us is a prosecutor, judge, and jury, and they all agree that the other person is wrong and we are right. This internal courtroom is happy to work overtime. It goes on hour after hour trying and prosecuting the person. This internal dialogue stops only when we sleep and then resumes early the next morning!

In addition to this internal courtroom, all our friends may agree that the other person has overstepped the boundaries. But despite all this sympathy, we are still miserable.

Why? Because being right has nothing to do with being happy. We can be right up, down, and across, but as long as we are angry, we have no internal peace. Sometimes, the other person apologizes to us, and we are still miserable. To be happy, we have to give up wanting to prove our case, give up needing to have the last word, give up craving to be vindicated. *The Eight Verses of Thought Transformation* says:

> When others, out of jealousy,
> Mistreat me with abuse, slander and so on,
> I will practice accepting defeat
> And offering the victory to them.

This verse does not mean that we naively capitulate in every conflict. Rather, seeing that the need to be right is simply a button, we choose to shut down the internal courtroom and send home the judge, jury, and prosecutor. We give up our anger because we see that it only harms us. "Offering the victory to them" simply means that we contract our over-sensitive buttons and cease obsessing about the incident.

For seven years Heather had not seen Ed, her ex-husband, and had never met his new wife, Gloria. They were coming in from another city to attend the graduation of Heather and Ed's daughter. The week before they were to arrive, Heather, who had always blamed the breakup on Ed, learned that he was complaining that he had gone into debt supporting the two children he had had with Heather. Heather was enraged, because she felt that, as a single mother, she had sacrificed tremendously and that Ed had given her too little and had given it reluctantly. Realizing that many of her buttons were being pushed, Heather called her friend for advice. Her friend recommended that she read a small booklet published by a Buddhist center, called "Working With Anger," and listen to the tapes of a talk on the topic. It took her friend a while to convince Heather to write down the name of the booklet and tapes, because Heather kept interrupting, "Yes, but I need to set the record straight with Ed immediately. I can't stand his lies!"

However, after reading the booklet and listening to the tapes, Heather felt she had some tools to deal with the situation, although she was not completely confident that she would be able to avoid blowing up and creating a scene when Ed and Gloria arrived. As it happened, at the airport Gloria had spilled something on her dress. Heather's daughter took it home and washed it, and seeing it crumpled, Heather ironed it before her daughter returned it to Gloria. A little kindness can dramatically change a situation. Heather felt good about ironing the dress and Gloria was touched by her generosity. When the two women met the next day, they were happy to see each other and embraced, much to everyone's surprise. Meanwhile, Heather let go of her resentment and thought, "The divorce was hard for both Ed and me. We both had to make adjustments and difficult sacrifices for the children. But I'm sure he is as happy as I am now watching our daughter graduate from college." Much to everyone's delight, the graduation festivities went well.

Let Go of the "Rules of the Universe"

All of us have "rules of the universe"—unconscious preconceptions that condition the way we view life. These include "Everything should happen the way I want it to," "Everyone should like and appreciate me," and "Everyone should agree with my opinions and do things my way." When we view others and the world through those preconceptions, we inevitably get into conflict with everyone and everything. We feel unappreciated, unloved, and discriminated against. This is not coming from others, but from our view of them. Once we recognize our false preconceptions are buttons and begin to dissolve them, we find the world a much nicer place. We are able to appreciate others and work for their benefit, without being disapproving or antagonistic towards them.

Several years ago, a group of people I respected and trusted broke the "rules of my universe" and unexpectedly interfered with a project on which I had diligently worked for months. As a result, much to my displeasure, the project was canceled. I had to admit I held animosity towards the group. I used Buddhist techniques for working with anger, and over time this diminished, but every so often it would flare up, and my "rules of the universe" would resurface, making me quite miserable. One day, in the middle of such a flare-up, I was walking to my room and suddenly the thought hit me, "This planet has six billion human beings on it, and no one else is as upset about this situation as I am. In fact, most people don't even know about it, and those that do aren't terribly concerned. If this event is so insignificant for all other sentient beings, why do I spend so much time focusing on it?" Since I clearly saw the foolishness of dwelling any longer on me and my concerns, my rancor fell away.

Discover the Real Issue

Because self-centeredness interprets events in relationship to "me," we not only become upset at others' comments but also exaggerate their import. For example, Martin and Karen had an agreement that he would shop for groceries and she would wash the dishes. One day at breakfast, Karen looked for peanut butter to put on her toast and not finding any, asked, "Honey, did you forget to buy the peanut butter?"

Still sleepy, Martin mumbled something, and feeling he didn't care, she said, "It's your job to do the shopping. We agreed on that."

"I know," he responded, "but it's no big deal. I'll get some next week when I go shopping."

But Karen felt brushed off, because she ate peanut butter most mornings and Martin knew that. "This happened last week, too. You waited until we were completely out of bagels before buying more. And last month, you went shopping and forgot to get margarine. You know, this situation happens over and over with us. You ignore your responsibilities and then, when I say something, you tune out. In fact, this is indicative of our whole marriage. You just don't care about me and you're totally irresponsible. In fact, I wonder if you love me and if this marriage is going to work!" By this time, Karen was fuming and left the breakfast nook in a huff. Martin, meanwhile, sat there dumbfounded, thinking, "My goodness, it was only peanut butter!"

This story—varieties of which are unfortunately often repeated—clearly shows how our mind creates our experience. When our buttons are pushed, we can make one event or phrase into the symbol of an entire relationship. Our mind builds on a small occurrence, making it into a huge one that we are certain is true. Upset, our mind jumps from one conclusion to another with astounding speed. In addition, we draw on our arsenal of stored painful experiences to lob onto the other person. We have collected this arsenal over time, accumulating all the small things our friend has done that we don't like. Rather than dropping them or clearing them up when they occur, we have stored them in our memory to use as ammunition the next time a fight occurs. Then we shell the other person with past situations that he or she may not remember.

How can we avoid this? First, by being aware of our feelings, we will notice anger when it is small and apply the antidotes to settle our mind. Then, depending on the situation, we may decide to explore the issue with the other person. In this way, we avoid stockpiling hurtful experiences that could build up resentment and lead to an explosion.

Second, by being aware of our feelings, we will learn to identify the real issue in the conflict, instead of being lead astray by false buttons, in this case the lack of peanut butter. We can ask ourselves whether we're upset by the ostensible issue (that there is no peanut butter) or whether we're really upset by the underlying issue (that we feel we're drifting away from the partner whom we care about). In this way, we will know whether we need to discuss the problem at hand (restocking the kitchen shelves) or something deeper (our mutual respect and concern for each other). Then, we can discuss the situation, being sure to listen carefully and to express ourselves in ways the other person can understand.

Chapter Ten

ACCEPTANCE AND EMPOWERMENT

Underneath our anger, we often find a refusal to accept the reality of a situation and a feeling of powerlessness in its face. These feelings are related, because the confusion that arises from fighting the reality of an event makes us feel helpless and unable to influence it. Once we accept what is happening, we can determine more clearly the parameters of possible action and feel empowered to act.

Accept What Is Happening

Often, we become angry because we think that someone shouldn't think, do, or say what they are or that things shouldn't happen the way they are. In other words, our mind does not accept the reality of whatever is happening and wants it to be different. We may develop many reasons why things should be different, but that doesn't change the reality of what they are.

Jackie ate a healthy diet and exercised, yet she was diagnosed with cancer at age forty-two. Her mind spun in disbelief, "I took such good care of my health. This can't happen to me!" Presupposing the worst, she fell into depression and did little to deal constructively with her illness. By attending a support group at the Wellness Center, Jackie came to accept that she had cancer. In addition, she met many others who had it and had survived. Their example encouraged her, and feeling more in control of the situation, she began to research various treatment options in order to make a wise decision. Feeling that she had some power to deal with the situation, she began taking better care of herself physically and mentally. When I met her several years later, she was in good health and told me that the cancer had made her grow in ways that she could not have imagined previously. "As strange as it may sound," she said, "I now see the cancer as a gift."

Some people think that acceptance means not trying to change the situation and fear that such an attitude could be used to support abuse or oppression. However, this is not the case. Acceptance simply means fully accepting that what is happening now is indeed happening, even if we do not like what it is. We stop fighting the reality of the present moment and let go of our anger. Nevertheless, we can still aspire and work towards improving the situation in the future. In fact, acceptance of the present enables us to think more clearly about effective means for influencing what occurs in the future.

Act or Relax

The great Indian sage Shantideva said:

> Why be unhappy about something
> If it can be remedied?
> And what is the use of being unhappy about something
> If it cannot be remedied?

If we face an unpleasant situation and can change it, why get angry? We can act and either extricate ourselves or improve the situation. On the other hand, if we cannot alter the situation, why get angry? There's nothing effective we can do, so we are better off relaxing. Becoming agitated only compounds our suffering.

This technique is also helpful if we worry a lot. We can ask ourselves, "Can I do something about this situation?" If the answer is yes, then there's no need to worry. We can act. If the answer is no, then there's no use for worry. We can relax, see what happens, and deal with the situation the best we can.

A high school teacher, Ben, prepared his students for the upcoming state exams as well as he could. As exam time approached, he began to worry about his students' performance. The students sensed his apprehension and became anxious themselves. Realizing the unproductive effect his uneasiness was having on them, he said to himself, "We have worked hard together all semester. They are good students and will do their best. I trust them and give them my caring support." He breathed deeply, relaxed, and spent the last few days before the exam cheerfully encouraging them. His students responded to his ease and did fine on the exams.

Discover Power

Feelings of helplessness often instigate anger: a child becomes angry when she feels helpless in meeting her parent's expectations; an ill person is irascible when he cannot control his surroundings; an employee defensively lashes out when his boss is unhappy with his work. In all these situations, a person who is unable to control certain circumstances angrily blames others for her unhappy feelings of powerlessness.

Interestingly, in most conflict situations, both parties feel that the other is more powerful. In the above examples, the parents feel helpless when their child acts out in frustration; the family members feel overwhelmed by the patient's abrasive speech; the manager is concerned that if the project deadline is not met, she will have to answer for her subordinate's inefficiency. Because we are interdependent, everyone in a situation affects the others. However, we are seldom aware that the person we consider powerful also is dependent on others and may at times feel helpless as well. Simply being aware of this can temper our anger and make the situation more manageable, because we will see ourselves not as helpless victims but as interdependent players.

Also, recognizing that feelings of helplessness may lie beneath anger, we can help others initiate action or initiate action ourselves that will affect the future in a positive way. This, too, can subdue anger. For example, when Shara, who used to be a happy, easygoing child began throwing temper tantrums, her parents took a serious look at their relationship to her. They realized that they had set extremely high standards for her and she felt pressured to meet these. They lessened their expectations and gave her tasks that she could easily accomplish. Instead of comparing her to "better" children, they re-enforced her unique talents. Then, seeing that she could do things her parents appreciated, Shara became more confident, and feeling less frustrated, she stopped acting out.

Suffering from terminal cancer, Rod would angrily ring the call button at all hours of the day and night and demand that his nurses and family members give him more pain medication, even when he had just had some. Tired of this, one nurse made it possible for Rod to administer the pain medication himself by pressing a button when he felt the need for more. Suddenly, the complaints stopped. Looking back on it, everyone realized that Rod's difficult behavior had been due to his not having control over any aspect of his situation. Once he had control over even one aspect—his pain medication—his feelings of powerlessness declined, and he became more relaxed and amenable to receiving help in other ways.

Dale's boss had called him in to say she was disappointed with his work. While some bosses help their subordinates improve in such situations, this one threatened him with a negative review if he didn't improve. Becoming defensive, Dale wanted to say something nasty, but he realized that doing so would only put his job even more at risk. Instead of wallowing in feelings of helpless dismay, he thought about the positive steps he could take to feel more powerful in the situation. He learned about his company's policy regarding warnings, citations, and review. He then went to see his manager again, and together they worked out and put in writing what Dale's job entailed and the method and criteria by which his work would be evaluated. Following this, they set a date to meet again to see how he was progressing. In addition, when Dale felt the need to express his frustration with his work situation, he spoke with friends outside work, who offered helpful suggestions. In this way, he avoided venting his feelings in front of his colleagues, which would have only stirred them up and created more tension in the office. Thus, Dale's initial anger, which stemmed from feeling powerless, vanished as he took active steps to improve his situation.

Have a Compassionate Heart

While sometimes we can gain more control in a situation, other times we cannot. Here mental transformation is crucial. After the communist Chinese invasion of Tibet, thousands of Tibetans were imprisoned.

Truly a powerless situation, being a political prisoner has shattered many people's lives. However, one monk, who was released after many years, finally escaped to the Tibetan community in exile in India. There His Holiness the Dalai Lama asked him, "What was your greatest fear while imprisoned?" The monk replied, "Losing my compassion." Instead of giving in to feelings of being oppressed and demeaned, this monk had cultivated compassion not only for the young Chinese soldiers who controlled every facet of his life, but also those in the communist government who commanded them to do so. His compassion had sustained him in an otherwise intolerable situation and enabled him to emerge from it with a kind heart he could offer to others.

Similarly, I receive letters from prisoners in the United States who are interested in learning to practice Buddhism. Although conditions in United States prisons are better than in Tibet, in some aspects they are more dangerous. Nevertheless, several inmates who have a regular meditation practice tell me that they are happy for the opportunity to practice in a prison environment. "There is always someone for whom we can generate love and compassion. We are surrounded by people whom we have the possibility to help in some big or small way," they say. Even those whom the policy of mandatory minimum sentencing has unjustly harmed accept their situation and use it to practice.

Terminal illness is another situation in which we lack control and could easily slip into feelings of powerlessness, depression, and anger. A natural outcome of life, death will happen to each of us, and acceptance, rather than rejection, of this facilitates our having a tolerable dying process and a peaceful death. One of my teachers, Lama Thubten Yeshe exemplified this. He literally had a hole in his heart, and his doctors could not believe he remained alive so long. In spite of his severe health condition, he was continuously cheerful and helpful to his numerous students. Those who cared for him after he became too debilitated to teach said that Lama maintained his focus on the well-being of others. He graciously accepted his continuously weakening condition and increasing dependence on others to help him with every facet of his life. Although he had little control of his physical condition, his mind was pacified, so that not only was he happy, but also he brought joy to those who cared for him.

Accept that Our Control Is Limited

Expecting to be happy and to be treated fairly, we feel that we have control or should have control over all that happens to us. But in fact, our control is limited. On the most basic level, although we can control some bodily functions, most of them are outside of our control. We become old, sick, and die without choice. Similarly, we have little control over our minds. Five minutes of trying to focus on our breath quickly reveals that our mind instead wanders here and there, and we are able to control it very little. If we cannot control the most basic elements of our experience—our body and mind—how can we possibly control what other people say and do? Yet we falsely think we should be able to.

Raising a child is a good example of how we are able to influence, but not control another person. Each parent does what she can to raise her children to have good values, a cheerful disposition, and behavior that enables them to get along well with others. Yet, children are not the parents' possessions. The parents cannot ensure that the child turns out the way they would like.

Our assumption that we should be able to control others is exposed as incorrect also when a relative or close friend has a substance-abuse problem. We feel that we should be able to confront the person with his self-destructive behavior and cause him to change. That, sadly, is not the case. We have to be there and help in a wise way however we can, but we cannot crawl inside another person and pull a few switches to alter his behavior and the attitudes motivating it.

From the Buddhist point of view, we are all trapped in cyclic existence by our own ignorance, anger, and clinging attachment. Ignorance misconceives the nature of reality by grasping onto ourselves and all phenomena as existing inherently and independently. This gives rise to our clinging to what gives us happiness and to our being hostile towards whatever interferes with this. These negative emotions, in turn, motivate confused actions that harm ourselves and others. Given this present state of affairs, our world is imperfect and we experience unhappiness. On the one hand, we would be happier if we stopped railing against the "unfairness of it all" and developed instead the tolerant ability to endure suffering, as long as its causes exist. On the other hand, we do not need to look forward to only more problems in life, for if we develop the determination and ability to eliminate their causes—ignorance, anger, and attachment—we can arrive at a state of lasting happiness, nirvana. Many people have done this before us. The path and the guides are there; we need only follow them.

Chapter Eleven

MEETING THE ENEMY

These days many people emphasize the importance of loving ourselves. From a Buddhist viewpoint, there are both positive and negative forms of self-love. Distinguishing them is critical for our well-being. The positive form of self-love wants what is best for ourselves and others in the long run. Seeing that we have the Buddha potential and the seeds of all positive qualities in our mindstream, it wants us to be free from all suffering forever and to attain the lasting happiness of liberation or enlightenment so that we can best help all others to realize that too. This self-love is the basis for valid and firm self-confidence. It makes our mind courageous in bearing short-term difficulties for the sake of attaining deep and long-lasting happiness for ourselves and others.

The negative form of self-love, on the other hand, thinks, "My happiness is more important than anyone else's. I've got to take care of myself first, for in this rough world, if I don't look out for my own welfare, who will?" Although most of us are too polite to state this publicly, if we check inside, we'll see that we generally live according to the thought "me and mine first." Our first thought in the morning—which frequently is "Where's my coffee?"—concerns our own short-term pleasure. All day long, we look out for our own happiness first, and before going to bed, we think, "Oh, bed. I'm so exhausted!" We aren't bad because we are self-centered, but if we look closely, we'll find that this view causes us innumerable problems, for we become overly sensitive to everything concerning the self. Because this form of self-interest pretends to be our friend and look out for our welfare, but in fact causes us difficulties, we call it negative.

We often consider other people as the source of our difficulties and say, "I have problems because my partner won't listen, my parents get on my case, my children don't appreciate me, the government is unfair, my boss is too critical," and so on. However, from the Buddhist viewpoint, our problems come primarily not from other sentient beings, but from the ignorance, anger, attachment, and self-centeredness in our own mind. Other people, through their kindness, enable us to stay alive, practice our spiritual path, and be happy. Only through their hard work do we have the things that sustain our life and bring us pleasure—our food, clothing, car, home, computer, sports equipment, books, and television.

Thus, while we usually consider our self-centeredness an asset that protects us and often see other people as hassles, if we look more closely, we will see that these roles are reversed: other sentient beings are kind, and our self-centeredness is the enemy.

Give the Pain to Our Self-Centeredness

As we become more aware of our thoughts and actions and their influence on ourselves and others, we'll notice that our self-centeredness causes many problems. It propels us to say and do things that hurt others. It enters almost every conflict we have with others: we want our way; we're convinced our idea is right. In addition, our selfish attitude is one of the biggest obstacles to gaining spiritual realizations because it causes us to be lazy in our practice. If we reflect deeply over time, we will become firmly convinced that our real enemy, what obstructs our happiness and well-being, is our self-centered attitude.

Although this is so, self-centeredness isn't an inherent part of us. It's like a thief in our house, and we can drive it out once we recognize its danger. From a Buddhist perspective, it's possible to separate the person from her attitude of unhealthy self-preoccupation.

Once we become convinced that self-centeredness is neither beneficial nor an inseparable part of us, we can take any pain we experience and give it to the selfish attitude. For example, when we don't like listening to another person's cutting remarks, we can think, "Great! I'll give all the pain and uncomfortable feelings to my selfish attitude. It's the real enemy, so let it be the target." This technique is not to be confused with blaming ourselves or assuming responsibility for things that aren't our doing. Here, we are differentiating between ourselves and the real troublemaker, our self-centered attitude. Then, because we want ourselves to be happy, we give the trouble to our self-centeredness.

If we do this practice properly and sincerely, then when someone criticizes or harms us, we'll be happy, not because we're masochistic, but because we've given the damage to the real enemy, our self-centeredness. Then, the more someone harms us, the happier we'll be! In fact, we'll think, "Come on, criticize me some more. I want my self-cherishing attitude to be harmed." This is a profound thought training technique. The first time I heard it, I thought, "This is impossible! What do you mean I'm supposed to be happy when someone criticizes me? How can I possibly practice this?"

But one time I did practice it, and the result was remarkable. I was on pilgrimage in Asia, travelling on horseback to a remote site. One day, something was wrong with my companion Henry's horse, so he had to walk, leading his horse by the reins. Henry was hungry and tired from the long journey, so walking was a burden to him. Since I felt okay, I offered him my horse.

I don't understand why, but this upset Henry. And, as often happens when a person becomes angry, Henry began remembering many things I'd done wrong over the years. He recited my faults from years ago and the problems I had caused other people. Here we were in this idyllic place, on pilgrimage to a holy site, and he went on and on, "You did this, and you did that. So many people complain about you."

I'm usually very sensitive to criticism and easily hurt, so I determined, "I'm going to give all this pain to my self-cherishing attitude." I meditated like this as we were walking along, and much to my surprise, I started thinking, "This is good! I really welcome your criticism. I'm going to learn from it. Thank you for helping to consume my negative karma by telling me my faults. All the pain goes to my selfish attitude because that's my real enemy. Tell me more."

When we finally set up camp for the evening and made tea, my mind was completely peaceful. I think this was the blessing of the pilgrimage because it proved to me that it is possible to be happy when unwished-for events occur. I didn't have to fall into my old habit of "Poor me."

See How the Enemy Benefits Us

To overcome our self-centeredness and anger, we can learn to regard an enemy as a friend who benefits us. We'll use the word "enemy" here to describe anyone with whom we don't get along at a particular moment. Even people for whom we deeply care can, then, become "enemies" when they act in ways that seem contrary to our interests, happiness, or welfare. Thus, we see in our lives that a person who is a friend today may become an enemy tomorrow if he does something of which we disapprove. He may return to being a friend the following day, once we have straightened out the misunderstanding.

How can we see an enemy as a friend? First, by harming us an enemy gives us the opportunity to practice giving our pain to our self-centeredness, as mentioned above. Second, by harming us an enemy makes our negative karma ripen, so that specific karma is now finished. Third, he forces us to examine our priorities and actions and decide what we want to do in the future. Thus, a person who harms us helps us grow. Indeed, the times of most intensive personal growth often occur when our sense of well-being and security has been shaken by someone harming us. We survive those difficult situations and emerge stronger and wiser as a result. Although such circumstances and the person who causes them are unpleasant, they enable us to discover resources—such as wisdom and compassion—within ourselves that we didn't know we had. From this perspective, one who harms us is kinder to us than a friend who doesn't offer us such challenges!

In fact, an enemy is kinder to us than the most compassionate being we can imagine, for example, the Buddha. This may sound almost inconceivable: "What do you mean my enemy is kinder to me than the Buddha? The Buddha has perfect compassion for everyone.

The Buddha doesn't harm a fly! How can my enemy who is such a jerk be kinder than the Buddha?"

We can look at it this way: To become Buddhas, we need to practice patience and tolerance. Doing this is essential; there's no other way to become a Buddha. Have you ever heard of an irritable or intolerant Buddha? But with whom can we practice patience? Not with the Buddha, because he doesn't upset us. Not with our friends, because they're nice to us. Who gives us the opportunity to practice patience? Who is so kind and helps us develop that infinitely good quality of patience? Only a person who harms us. Only our enemy. That is why our enemy is kinder to us than the Buddha.

My teacher made this very clear to me when I was an assistant director of an institute. The director, Sam, and I didn't get along at all. In fact, an independent American woman working together with a macho Italian man created something akin to Los Alamos. During the day, I would get angry at him, and in the evening I would go back to my room and think, "I blew it again," and for help pull out Shantideva's *A Guide to the Bodhisattva's Way of Life*. Finally I left that job and went to Nepal, where I saw my teacher, Zopa Rinpoche. We were sitting on the roof of his house, looking at the Himalayas, so peaceful and calm, when Rinpoche asked me, "Who's kinder to you, Sam or the Buddha?"

I thought, "You've got to be kidding! There's no comparison. The Buddha is obviously so kind, but Sam is another case!" So I replied, "The Buddha, of course."

Rinpoche looked at me as if to say, "Wow! You still haven't gotten the point!" and said, "Sam gave you the opportunity to practice patience. The Buddha didn't. You can't practice patience with the Buddha, and you need to perfect the quality of patience to become enlightened. Therefore, Sam is kinder to you than the Buddha."

I sat there dumbfounded, trying to digest what Rinpoche had said. I had expected him to say something different, such as, "I know Sam is a difficult person, and you did so well putting up with him all that time." But, no, consolation and praise for my ego were not in store. Instead, my teacher confronted me with my intolerance.

Slowly, as the years have gone by, the meaning of what he said has sunk in and changed me. Now when I see Sam, I appreciate what I learned from him and regret that, at the time, I was not able to benefit from working with him. It has also subsequently occurred to me that maybe I wasn't the easiest person with whom to work!

Bodhisattvas, those beings dedicated to becoming Buddhas in order to benefit all sentient beings most effectively, are happy when someone harms them, for they are eager to practice patience and now have the opportunity to do so. But being imbued with love and compassion, bodhisattvas have a hard time finding anyone who appears disagreeable or who feels hostile towards them. We ordinary beings, on the other hand, often perceive others as obnoxious and seek out those who will treat us nicely. Despite this, so many people feel, "I can't find anyone to love me." Bodhisattvas, however, say, "I can't find anyone to hate me!"

Remember the Potential Goodness of the Enemy

To prevent anger from rising in response to harm we can also ask ourselves, "Is it this person's nature to harm us?" In one way, we can say it is human nature to mistreat others upon occasion. We're all sentient beings caught in the net of cyclic existence, so of course our minds are obscured by ignorance, anger, and attachment. If that's our present situation, why expect ourselves or others to be free of misconceptions and destructive emotions? If a person is harmful by nature, then getting angry at him is useless. It would be like getting angry at fire because its nature is to burn. That's just the way fire is; that's just the way this person is. Becoming upset about it is senseless because that cannot alter the cause of the injury.

On the other hand, if a person is not harmful by nature, there's no use getting angry at him. His inconsiderate behavior is extraneous; it's not his nature. From a Buddhist perspective, the deepest nature of even the people who have acted most horrendously is not harmful. They, too, have the pure Buddha potential, the pure nature of their mind, which is their real nature. Their destructive behavior is like a thundercloud temporarily obscuring the clear sky. That behavior is not intrinsic to them, so why make ourselves miserable by being angry at what is not really them? Thinking this way is extremely helpful.

We must separate the person from her behavior. We can say a particular behavior, such as cheating or lying, is harmful, but we cannot say the person who does it is evil. That person, like everyone else, has the Buddha potential. She can, and one day will, become a fully enlightened being. Her negative action was motivated by disturbing attitudes and destructive emotions, which are like clouds obscuring the pure nature of her mind. They are not her nature; neither they nor her actions define who she is as a human being.

Sometimes a part of us feels comfortable categorizing people: Adolf Hitler was evil. End of discussion. But how do we feel inside when we label another living being as inherently evil? And what does that say for us when we err and harm others? Do we also then become irredeemably evil?

The Rodney King episode several years ago brought this point home to me. I thought, "If I were raised like King, who drove dangerously fast on a highway to avoid being pulled over, I probably would have acted as he did. If I were raised like the police officers who beat him, I could have behaved like them. If I were brought up as the Korean grocers were, I could have acted similarly, and if I lived in the circumstances of those who rioted, I could have done that too. When I honestly looked at myself, placed in suitable conditions, I could have thought like any of those people and done any of those actions. Fortunately, I have not been in those situations, but I am not totally free from the potential to act as they did. I cannot arrogantly condemn them as evil if I haven't eliminated the seeds of those emotions and behaviors within me. For this reason, compassion for ourselves and others is appropriate and essential.

While compassion does not approve of or condone harmful actions, it does have a kind attitude towards the sentient beings who mistakenly commit them. It doesn't omit any sentient being from its scope, no matter what he does, because underneath his pain and confusion, each sentient being is just like us—he wants only to be happy and be free from suffering. Furthermore, compassion is optimistic. It knows that because people are not inherently evil, they can improve and their dreadful actions can stop.

Repay Hostility with Kindness

Another way to deal with our anger at an enemy is to do the reverse of what we feel like doing. While our angry mind generally wants to retaliate by harming the other, changing our attitude and showing kindness is more beneficial for ourselves and for others. We can be kind without capitulating to others' unreasonable demands.

Once upon a time, a monster asked to see the emperor. Rebuked by the emperor's secretaries, the monster forced his way into the emperor's reception room, where the ministers were assembled, waiting for the emperor. The ministers panicked and began to hurtle abuse at the monster in an attempt to force him to leave. "You're ugly!" ridiculed one. "You're useless," insulted another. "You're evil," condemned a third. With each insult, the monster grew bigger and meaner, until his repulsive body and negative energy filled the room, terrifying the ministers.

At that point, the emperor walked in. A wise person, he knew that using verbal abuse fuels one's own anger and seldom intimidates the other; indeed it usually inflames him. Speaking in a soothing voice to the monster, then, the emperor said, "You're welcome here, friend. Please sit down and have a cup of tea. Would you like some cookies too?" With each kind remark, the monster grew smaller and less threatening, until he was quite docile and sweet. At that point, the emperor asked him, "What did you come here to speak to me about?" and they had a friendly chat. The ministers meanwhile stood by, surprised by the transformation in the monster and remorseful due to their own stupidity for antagonizing him.

We too need to speak kindly to those we fear or find repulsive. As it says in *The Eight Verses of Thought Transformation:*

> Whenever I meet a person of bad nature,
> Who is overwhelmed by negative energy and suffering,
> I will hold such a rare one dear,
> As if I had found a precious treasure.

One morning, Joe noticed that his car, which was parked in front of his house, was scratched. The paint on the scratch matched that of his neighbor's car, but when he asked his neighbor about it, the old man indignantly denied any involvement. Joe had the car repaired, but a few weeks later saw another scratch of the same color; his neighbor again defensively denied any involvement. Joe was at a loss. He didn't want his car continually scratched, nor did he relish living next door to someone so disagreeable.

Discussing the situation with some friends one evening, he asked for their suggestions. They toyed with various plans but none seemed to relieve Joe of his negative feelings. Finally, one said, "What would our spiritual teacher do in this situation?" to which another replied, "He'd give the man a present."

After an initial groan, Joe considered the idea further and decided to try it. Knowing that the old man was an avid golfer, he bought him some new golf balls, which he had gift-wrapped. The neighbor reluctantly opened his door when Joe rang the bell, looked suspicious when Joe with a sincere smile said, "I'd like you to have this," and slammed the door when Joe left.

A half-hour later, the old man appeared at Joe's door, his face totally transformed. Radiant, he said to Joe, "I've experienced much suffering in my life and little happiness. Thank you for being one who has contributed to my happiness."

Another example of the value of changing our attitude and showing kindness occurred when I was leading a retreat on Mother's Day weekend. On Saturday a couple approached me for advice. They explained that their son had recently divorced his wife, who was very bitter about the separation. They feared that, as revenge, their ex-daughter-in-law would deny them the ability to visit their two grandchildren, whom they dearly loved. They considered taking her to court if need be and asked my advice. I suggested, "Before deciding what to do, first try to release you suspicion and ill-will towards her. She is already hurt, and if you approach her ready to argue, she will detect that in you and reply accordingly. You already know the ugly scene that will result, and I'm sure you don't want your grandchildren to undergo years of antagonism between their mother and grandparents." The couple nodded. They were with me, so I continued, "You have two beautiful grandchildren due to the kindness of your daughter-in-law. Without her, they would not have been born. She has raised them and enabled them to become who they are, and for all that you have to be thankful. Mother's Day is tomorrow. You may want to consider sending her flowers and say, 'Thank you for being the mother of our grandchildren.' Let her know that you appreciate her for that, and see what happens."

The couple was surprised by the suggestion, and I hope they followed it. My guess is that their daughter-in-law would respond positively, but even if she did not, their attitude would have changed and become more positive towards her, releasing them from the stress of malice.

Chapter Twelve

LETTING GO OF GRUDGES AND RESENTMENT

To transform our anger, we must apply these techniques to actual situations. During our meditation or reflection times, we can recall our painful experiences and consider them in light of these techniques. We all have a reservoir of grudges that we still hold against others. Instead of suppressing them, we can draw them out and reframe them. In this way, we'll be able to let go of lingering hurt and resentment. If we don't do this, we will hold grudges for years, and sometimes die with them. We make ourselves miserable by carefully guarding these memories, never forgetting the harm we received.

Holding grudges serves no productive purpose. It eats at us like mental cancer. The other person harmed us once or twice—a fixed number of times—in the past. Yet each day, when we remember the harm and become hurt or angry about it, we harm ourselves again. In this way, holding grudges becomes an excellent form of self-torture.

In addition, holding grudges can result in our taking revenge on others. If we do succeed in retaliating and causing someone pain in return, we have difficulty respecting ourselves later. We don't feel our dignity as human beings when we delight in deliberately harming others.

It may take a while to free our minds from grudges that we have held for years. Replacing habitual resentment with habitual patience takes time and consistent effort. Of course, prevention is the best medicine. Rather than having to let go of anger built up over time, it's wiser to calm our own mind and communicate with the other person early on and thus stop the proliferation of misunderstandings.

If we do allow our anger to build up over time, how can we blame our being angry on the other person? We have some responsibility to deal with our anger effectively right away.

Avoid Cultivating Grudges

Families, as well as people in tightly knit communities, excel at holding grudges. I know an extended family that purchased two houses for summer holidays on one piece of property. One day, the relatives in one house quarreled with those in the other, and their families—including those who were not yet born at the time of the initial quarrel—haven't spoken to each other since. Yet, they go to the houses in the summer to "relax and enjoy." If we asked these people if they wanted their children to be harmonious after they, the parents, passed away, I'm sure they would say yes. Yet, their behavior with their own siblings has provided a model for the opposite to occur. By holding grudges against one another, these people have sent the message to their children that this attitude and behavior is acceptable. As a result, within each successive generation, siblings have quarreled and stopped speaking to each other.

Let's look at the grudges we have held for years: a small incident happened—someone didn't attend a wedding or funeral, or someone embarrassed us in front of others—and we vowed never to speak to or be civil to that person again. We keep such vows perfectly, whereas we renegotiate our vows to avoid stealing and lying when it suits our self-interest.

Similarly, specific grudges and the acceptability of ostracizing those to whom we're close are passed from generation to generation within ethnic groups and nations. A joke is told about a Mother Superior who sent her postulates out to raise funds for the nunnery. When they returned, the most successful one was asked by the Abbess how she did it. She said, "Mother, I must confess. I became a prostitute." Hearing this, the Abbess fainted. When she regained consciousness, she said, "What did you become?" to which the younger nun said, "A prostitute." The Abbess sighed with relief and said, "Whew! I thought you said a Protestant!" Fortunately, the animosity between Catholics and Protestants is less these days, but the joke il-lustrates a grudge that has affected Western Civilization for centuries.

No one doing the killing in recent years in the former Yugosla-via was alive at the time the various parties initially quarreled several centuries ago. The deaths of massive numbers of people have occurred due to grudges passed down from parent to child for generations. Reflecting on their own lives, parents must think carefully, "What do I want to pass on to my children?" Then they should check their own attitudes and actions to see if they are modeling what they truly want their children to learn.

Understand Why Others Harm Us

When people harm us, instead of holding a grudge or seeking re-venge, we must understand that they harm us because they want to be happy and to avoid pain. They may use confused methods to ac-tualize this, but in the context of their own suffering and confusion, they are simply seeking a way to be happy. Examining our own lives, we see that we have acted similarly. That is, wishing happiness but feeling pain, we have used unproductive means that have harmed others in an attempt to be happy. We all have made cruel remarks to others directly as well as behind their backs, and we have even lied in our misinformed attempt to be happy. Looking back on those situ-ations, we can have compassion for the person we were when we did that, because we know how much we were hurting at the time. We can then bring the same degree of understanding and compassion to all those who have harmed us.

People harm others only when they are unhappy. No one wakes up in the morning and says, "I feel so great today! I think I'll go out and harm someone!" When we can allow ourselves to know the depth of the pain and confusion felt by those who have harmed us, compassion—the wish that they be free from such suffering—can easily arise. Thinking in this way does not mean whitewashing or denying harm that was done. Rather, we acknowledge it, but go beyond amassing resentment, because we know that grudges help neither ourselves nor others.

Remember Our Commonality with Others

Many of our grudges involve major episodes in our lives, such as abuse, battering, divorce, breach of trust, or financial deception. They may also involve being the recipient of racial, ethnic, religious, gender, homophobic, or class prejudice. These wrongs exist; we have to deal with them. We also have to see how we perpetrate them upon others. I have found that we are always extraordinarily aware of others' unfair biases about us and equally blind to our prejudices against them. If compassion doesn't move us to relinquish our preconceptions, understanding the functioning of karma and its effect will enable us to see that every time we harm others mentally, verbally, or physically, we are in fact bringing misery to ourselves.

Not all of our resentment concerns such major issues, however. Much of it relates to more minor events that we concretize and hold onto. As we reflect more and become more aware of what goes on in our mind and heart, we detect subtler levels of resentment. I had to laugh when, on a retreat, I realized I was still unhappy with my second grade teacher because she wouldn't let me be in the class play!

We may not realize that we are harboring a grudge until we notice that something inside of us recoils when we hear a particular person praised or know that we'll see him today. Generally, our mind sees such responses as justified because we've decided that the person really isn't such a reliable, trustworthy, or capable person anyway, and we don't look into it further. We simply tell ourselves, "I just don't like that person!" However, even such small grudges contract our heart and make us miserable. Think about it—we may have many good reasons for not liking someone and many people may agree with us—but does that make us happy?

We needn't like everyone; people have different dispositions and personalities and we may have more shared interests with some or feel closer to them than to others. However, we need to explore why we block some people out of our heart, feeling distaste, jealousy, or unease around them, all the while attributing it to the way *they* are, as if it had nothing to do with us and how we view them.

When we look inside, we may find many more opinions and prejudices than we would care to admit. We don't have to agree with or like whatever others do, but being judgmental or hostile helps neither ourselves nor them. When others don't do things I like, I remind myself that "sentient beings do sentient being things." In other words, here are beings who want happiness, don't want misery, and are confused about how to achieve this, just like me. Just as I cut myself some slack, I should similarly be patient with them.

Remembering that everyone without exception wants happiness and seeks to be free of suffering enables us to care about others whether we like them or not. When we look into others' hearts with this awareness, the petty dislikes and prejudices disappear. Instead, we feel an important common bond with them, for we understand something essential about them.

In addition, by remembering that our happiness depends on the kindness of others, our petty grievances evaporate. More than any other time in human history, we are dependent on others for everything we use and all that we know. We are not independent, isolated units, but live in relationship to everyone on the planet. For this reason, affection for others, simply because they are part of the world that sustains us is appropriate.

Forgive Others

As long as we hold onto our resentment, we can never forgive others, and our lack of forgiveness hurts no one but ourselves. To heal from our pain, there's no other alternative but to let go of our anger and forgive others. Forgiving simply means that we stop tying up our life's energy in being angry at a person. It does not mean saying their behavior was acceptable. We can still deem certain behavior to be wrong, injurious, or inappropriate. Forgiving also doesn't mean being naive, letting others manipulate us, or ignoring problems. We can forgive an alcoholic for being drunk, but that does not mean we expect him to remain sober from now on. We can forgive a person for lying to us, but in the future, it would be prudent to check her words.

We can forgive a spouse for having an extra-marital affair, but we shouldn't ignore the problems that prompted this behavior.

Often we find it difficult to forgive others' mistakes. But we too have made mistakes. Looking at our own behavior, we notice that sometimes we were overcome by disturbing attitudes and acted in ways that we later regretted. We want others to understand and forgive our mistakes—why, then, not let ourselves forgive theirs?

Telling ourselves we *should* forgive others does no good: we must actively apply an antidote. To do this, we must take out our old grudges and consider their pain, but without rerunning any self-pitying videos in our mind. We should then look at the old situations from a fresh perspective by employing the various techniques for dissolving anger already described. In this way, we'll release hostility that we've carried in our hearts for years.

When others offer an apology, we should accept it and avoid dwelling on the wrong they did. If we continue to hold a grudge after someone has apologized, we torment ourselves, and if we retaliate, we harm them. What use is either of these? Vengefully inflicting misery on others cannot undo the past. This doesn't mean that accepting another's apology will instantly free us from all of the ramifications of his or her behavior. However, it can release us from bitterness and hostility.

I met a eighty-year-old woman who, by a fluke, came to know that her husband had been cheating on her for years when their children were young. She told him of her finding and her pain at discovering his infidelity decades later, and he admitted his wrongdoing. She told me, "Initially it was hard to forgive him; but we've been married for sixty years, and I don't want him to die with my hatred on his back, and I don't want to die with it in my heart." She released her hurt and anger, he let go of his shame, and they continued to live together peacefully.

Chapter Thirteen

WHEN TRUST IS BETRAYED

The betrayal of trust is a very painful emotional experience, which occurs in many kinds of relationships. For example, our partner or spouse leaves us. Our children don't recognize how much we love them or how much we want to help them and instead turn their back on us with resentment. An employee whom we have trained doesn't care that we are relying on him and quits when we need him the most. Our boss doesn't appreciate our loyalty to the company and lays us off with the next budget cut. A close friend with whom we've shared the ups and downs of life for years suddenly talks behind our back and accuses us of using her. The list could go on and on. We have all had the experience of feeling betrayed by others. And yet, when it happens to us, the feelings are so powerful that we're sure no one has ever been treated this poorly or felt this badly. We easily get locked into our pain and grief, retreating inward or exploding outward in an attempt to eliminate the pain. In actual fact, however, everyone has experienced betrayal of trust. Our experience is not unique.

As painful as it is when our trust has been betrayed, we seldom think of ourselves as having betrayed others' trust. Yet, if each of us has experienced this, who has caused it? If we look deeply, we may find that each of us has intentionally or unintentionally betrayed others' faith in us. Although we should avoid feeling guilty and despising ourselves for this, it helps our own healing to admit that just as we were confused and miserable when we hurt others, they too were confused and miserable when they hurt us.

See the One Who Harms Us as Our Supreme Teacher

Buddhist teachings contain several methods for dealing with the anger and other painful emotions that arise when our trust is betrayed. *The Eight Verses of Thought Transformation* recommends dealing with this situation as follows:

> When someone I have benefited
> And in whom I have placed great trust
> Hurts me very badly,
> I will practice seeing that person as my supreme teacher.

At first reading, this verse seems almost impossible to practice. When we've been hurt, the last thing we want to do is see the other as our supreme teacher. Instead, we would rather belittle that person, telling others how unreliable and cruel he is. Some of us lash out in anger, seeking to hurt the other as much as she has hurt us. Others of us sink into despair and self-pity, holding on to our view that the world is a hostile place where there is no one upon whom we can rely.

However, when someone betrays us, we have the opportunity to learn profound lessons that we might not have otherwise realized. For example, if we look closely, we may learn that although we thought we sincerely wished the other person well, we may have expected him to meet our needs. Wishing another well is rooted in genuine caring; it is focused on the other person. Wanting someone to meet our needs is based on fixed ideas of who someone is and what he should do; it centers on us. This self-focused attitude predisposes us to disappointment later. When we finally realize this, we see that the person who hurts us is our supreme teacher, for he shows us the defects of our view, thus enabling us to revise it.

Inspect Our Unrealistic Expectations

To resolve our hurt and anger over a betrayal of trust, we need to acknowledge any grief that arises. In doing so, we sometimes will see what our own unrealistic expectations have been. For example, although we knew a person had problems, we still hoped these would disappear, especially since he had come to know us and we were helping him. Although we suspected someone was lying, we deluded ourselves into believing her because we wanted what she said to be true. Although we knew that so much of what happens in life cannot be controlled, we felt as if there should be someone who could fix it after we complained to them about the unfairness of it all. Letting these misconceptions surface and releasing them is an important step in the growth that comes from grieving in a healthy way.

Creating realistic expectations is an elusive art, for determining the point at which they become unrealistic is difficult. When we hire someone to do a job and he agrees, we expect him to abide by the agreement. However, if we concretize our expectation and do not accept that factors beyond our or his control may arise, we will run into trouble. When we recognize and let go of our concrete vision, our mind will be more fluid, and we will be able to gracefully accept what happens.

Rejoice in a Positive Past

When we've shared positive experiences with someone and later feel betrayed, we grieve not the loss of what we've had but the loss of the future of which we dreamed, which we now feel will never happen. Understanding this can be extremely helpful. The happiness and affection we shared in the past cannot be taken away. We have already experienced this and do not grieve its loss. Rather, we had visions and expectations of future happiness that we now realize will not be actualized, and we grieve this. But in looking more deeply, isn't it strange to grieve for what doesn't and never will exist, or to put it another way, to grieve for what existed only in our conceptual mind, in our imagination? Here we can clearly see the power of our mind in creating our experience, and thus the value of transforming our mind in order to reshape our experience.

We can prevent ourselves from getting stuck in our feelings of loss and betrayal if we rejoice in the goodness we were able to share with the other person in the past, instead of focusing on the craving to recreate it in the future and the disappointment of not being able to do so. Then, we can stop clinging to the other person and wish him well in whatever he encounters. We can make aspirational prayers that both of us progress along the path so that our lives become meaningful for ourselves and others.

Accept that Change is Universal

Grieving essentially means adapting to change. Although change is universal, we typically know this only intellectually. In the recesses of our mind, we grasp at permanence and predictability and feel that our trust has been betrayed when change that we did not predict and sanction happens. For example, we understand that our relationships are impermanent by their very nature. Everything that arises also changes. Thus, from the very beginning, any relationship by its nature is bound to change. There is no way around this. Yet unless we deeply accept this, we will be surprised when it does so.

Being Buddhist practitioners, Theresa and David had discussed the unpredictability of cyclic existence, although they never anticipated it would manifest the way it did in their friendship. They enjoyed each other's company, especially the Dharma discussions that enriched both of their practices. Nevertheless, as will happen, one day their egos arose and clashed, painful things were said back and forth, and both of them felt hurt, misunderstood, and angry. At that time, Theresa wrote to David:

"Our friendship has been stimulating and mutually beneficial. Yet, because both of us still have the seeds of confusion and anger in our minds, for sure one day we would quarrel. Previously we discussed our individual problems with anger and felt closer to each other because of it. Now that our anger is directed at each other, we need to go beyond our feelings of betrayal and deal with this change constructively. I've heard it said that someone does not truly become your friend until you have resolved at least three quarrels in a satisfactory way. So this is our chance.

"Both of us want happiness and neither of us wants suffering. I know, and I believe you do too, that both of us want the other to be happy, and neither of us wants the other to suffer. Yet, because we are beings under the influence of ignorance, this misunderstanding has occurred. In the moment, you may have meant the words you said, or I may simply have misunderstood you due to my buttons. The same may apply for your hearing what I said. It hardly matters who meant what. We each interpreted the other's words in a way that left us feeling hurt and angry. We both must work on ourselves to bring some gentleness into our minds. But I have confidence that due to the power of the Dharma and our commitment to it, we will both grow from this experience and that what initially appears to separate us will, in the end, enable us to oppose old habits and to grow in beneficial ways."

Reading this, David came to feel what Theresa had felt when she wrote it—that a strong basis for friendship existed and that both of them had the integrity to acknowledge, be responsible for, and modify what they had contributed to the disagreement. In time, by working on themselves, listening to each other closely, and communicating well, they were able to work things out. What could have remained a painful betrayal of trust had become the condition for individual growth and strengthening of their relationship.

Recognize the Nature of Cyclic Existence

It is helpful to recognize that being let down is part of the very nature of cyclic existence. Suffering and disappointment are bound to happen because we are under the influence of disturbing attitudes, negative emotions, and karma. Why be surprised when they do? Being aware of the nature of cyclic existence in this way will propel us to eliminate its causes by practicing the Dharma.

Meanwhile, we can recognize that others are under the influence of disturbing attitudes and negative emotions just as we are. Why should we expect ordinary sentient beings similar to ourselves to be continuously kind and clear in their motivation and actions? They, as we, are frequently overpowered by prejudice, misjudgment, fear, and greed. When they do or say things that hurt us, they are doing so because they are unhappy.

Letting go of expectations and recognizing the nature of cyclic existence do not entail becoming cynical. Derisively thinking "I can't expect anything of anyone" is not a virtuous or realistic attitude that helps us on the path to enlightenment! Even though others have let us down, we can still hold the aspiration that their minds will be clearer and their actions more consistent in the future. The person still has the Buddha potential, and we pray that she will be able to actualize it. In that way, our mind remains optimistic and hopeful regarding the future.

Look at Our Situation from a Wider Perspective

We need to put our suffering in perspective. We generally feel that the betrayal of our trust is unfair. "The world should treat me better!" says our self-centered attitude. However, if we compare the injustice we experience with the injustice that others in the world experience, ours is likely to be relatively minor. Most of us are not refugees due to political circumstances beyond our control. We are not on death row for crimes we did not commit. We are not being lynched or put in a concentration camp. Looking at our situation from this wider perspective, our mind becomes stronger and more capable of bearing the suffering. Of course, we must still oppose injustice, but we can do so with compassion free from self-centered anger.

Considering the unpleasant and unwished for situation we are experiencing as a result of our own karma helps our mind remain calm. Blaming others for our suffering is a dead end, for we can never control others' behavior. Instead of giving our power away by thinking our happiness depends on the other person, we can regard our own previously created actions to be the real reason for our being in this situation. People betray our trust and hurt us because we did the same to others either in this or previous lives. At first we may not like to hear this, but when we think about it, who among us has not deliberately hurt someone else's feelings? Since we all have, why are we so surprised when we receive back what we have given to others? This point of view empowers us, because if our past harmful actions have resulted in our difficult present situations, then our present actions—which we can choose to make positive—can result in a happy future.

From the wider perspective that includes previous lives, we may even come to be glad that the present difficulty has happened, for now the negative karmic imprint causing it has been expended and no longer obscures our mind. We can rejoice that this karmic imprint didn't ripen in an even more severe result.

Chapter Fourteen

THE SNAKE OF ENVY

The First Dalai Lama, Gedundrup, said:

> Attached to its dark hole of ignorance,
> It cannot bear seeing the wealth and excellence of others,
> But quickly fills them with its vicious poison,
> The snake of envy—save us from this danger!

A form of anger, envy is indeed like a poisonous snake. It is a mental factor that, out of attachment to respect and material gain, is unable to bear the good things that others have.

Like a snake, envy is sneaky, winding its way into areas we may not suspect. While we frequently envy others' wealth, relationship, or status, we can also be jealous of their good qualities, for example their skill in basketball or computers. The jealous mind may follow us also into spiritual practice. We may resent someone who can sit in the meditation position longer, has done more retreats, has a closer relationship with the teacher, or has had more extraordinary spiritual experiences than we. We may begrudge someone who appears more virtuous or has a greater positive influence on others than we, and seek to denigrate him and cause others to lose faith in him.

See the Disadvantages of Envy

The Buddha taught various ways to tame the snake of envy. First, clearly seeing the disadvantages of jealousy gives us the impetus to abandon it, thus eliminating our own pain and preventing our inflicting suffering on others. Under the influence of envy, our mind is in turmoil—we fear that others will have what we want—and sometimes we are unable to eat or sleep properly. Our own good qualities are ignored and exhausted as we seek to invalidate or obliterate others' talents, success, or good fortune. In this way, our friendships are destroyed, as we slander, denigrate, and gossip about others. People's happiness is destroyed and their feelings hurt; innocent parties are dragged into taking sides in the conflict that ensues. Our actions plant destructive karmic seeds in our mindstream, creating the causes for our encountering difficulties in future lives and obscuring our mind so that we don't gain realizations of the path to enlightenment. In short, envy prevents all worldly and spiritual happiness from coming our way.

At one time or another, each of us has been under the sway of jealousy that seeks to harm others. We know from our own experience how painful that emotion is, even when we do not act it out by physically or verbally attacking someone. It is even more painful when it provokes us to destroy another's happiness or rejoice in her misfortune. By celebrating or causing another person's pain, we relinquish our own self-respect. As Shantideva said:

> Even if your enemy is made unhappy
> What is there for you to be joyful about?
> Your merely wishing (for him to be hurt)
> Did not cause him to be injured.

> And even if he does suffer as you had wished,
> What is there for you to be joyful about?
> If you say, "For I shall be satisfied,"
> How could there be anything more wretched than that?

Jason was jealous of his sister who, in his eyes, was more successful than he. He continuously put her down and tried to prove himself, especially at family gatherings. This embarrassed her, made others lose respect for him, and ruined family harmony. He reached a point where the jealousy was so intense that he had to acknowledge his pain and decided to change. He stopped comparing himself to his sister, and realizing that each of them had their own individual talents, he focused on developing his.

Jealousy does not bring us what we desire. For example, whether or not our rival has a wonderful relationship does not change the fact that we lack one. Our skiing skill remains the same whether someone else is better or worse than we. When we reflect deeply in this way, we see that envy has no rational basis. Comparing ourselves to others with a jealous mind only makes us miserable. As Shantideva commented:

> What does it matter if (my enemy) is given something or not?
> Whether he obtains it
> Or it remains in the benefactor's house,
> In either case, I shall get nothing.

Change Our Motivation to Wishing Others Happiness

Recognizing that jealousy contradicts our wishes for happiness stimulates us to change our perspective. In the above example, Jason consciously began to change his motivation from making himself look good to being of service to others. As his orientation changed, so did his behavior, making everyone in the family happy.

While we all want to be happy, our mind often prevents itself from being happy. For example, we cannot endure others' being praised and instead crave recognition for ourselves. As Shantideva commented:

> When people describe my own good qualities
> I want others to be happy too.
> But when they describe the good qualities of others
> I do not wish to be happy myself.

We often say, especially in season's-greetings cards, "May all beings be happy." Therefore, we should be pleased when others are praised, honored, or wealthy, particularly if we didn't have to exert any energy to bring about their happiness. But at times, contrary to our wish for peace and happiness on Earth, when another has even some small good fortune, we cannot endure it! In such situations, we need to remind ourselves of our real wish and abandon the envy which makes us unhappy when another's desire is fulfilled.

Don't Envy What Doesn't Bring Lasting Happiness (or Even What Does)

The things we envy in others do not bring lasting happiness. Even the richest or most famous people in our society must still age, fall ill, and eventually die. They cannot find protection in their wealth, fame, or good qualities, nor can they take those things with them at death. In addition, they have many problems that others do not. For example, while others have the freedom to walk in the park with their family, movie stars and billionaires have lost all anonymity and cannot do this. Fearing that their children will be kidnapped, they cannot send their children to school. If we had the opportunity to talk to the people we envied, we would soon hear their problems and realize that they are not really any happier than we are.

What antidote can we apply when we envy those with spiritual realizations, which do bring lasting happiness? We can ask ourselves what good it does to want them to be bereft of these? People who develop love and compassion work for the benefit of all beings, including ourselves, so by begrudging them their kind heart, generosity, and wisdom, we harm ourselves. It serves our happiness, as well as theirs, to rejoice in their attainments.

Rejoice that Others Are Better than We Are

Being happy that others are better than we is an excellent antidote to jealousy. While we usually want to be the best ourselves, we have to admit that if we were the best, with just our current abilities, the world would lack a great deal. For example, if I were the best this world had to offer, we would not have electricity, plumbing, cars, computers, or even food, for I know nothing about how to produce these. Since everything I use and enjoy in life is dependent on others' skills, I rejoice that they have those talents and use them well.

In addition, even in our area of specialty, we can rejoice if others are more knowledgeable and capable than we are. With them to teach us, we can advance more easily, and our own abilities are stimulated. Therefore, rejoicing in others' capabilities and success is appropriate.

Also, rejoicing in others' abilities takes the pressure off ourselves to "be best," a goal that is increasingly difficult to attain and hold onto in this age of rapid communication. Previously, each village had its own "best singer" and "best carpenter," for example. Now all these "best" people compete with each other for worldwide fame. Thus, only a very few are selected and idolized and their fame is more short-lived than ever, with so many newcomers continually joining the competition.

Furthermore, we would have to admit that if we were the best with just our current abilities, or even with our abilities suddenly surpassing those of the others we now envy, still we would experience no lasting happiness. We would be fraught with the anxiety of maintaining that position, all the time being aware that one day we would have to relinquish it because all things change. Thinking in this way can help us release our envy and rejoice in others' talents for whatever contribution they are making at present.

Rejoice in Others' Good Fortune and Excellent Qualities

Rejoicing is an attitude that appreciates and enjoys others' happiness, talents, wealth, knowledge, skills, and virtue. Whereas envy cannot endure others' good fortune and excellent qualities, rejoicing appreciates these, thus filling our mind with joy. Of course, when we are in the throes of jealousy, we must make some effort to broaden our mind and rejoice, and if we do, many benefits accrue.

For example, one student told me of seeing his ex-girlfriend's new boyfriend in the supermarket. At first, Phil was tempted to ignore him and leave, but remembering his fledgling rejoicing meditation at a recent retreat, he decided to approach him instead. Before doing so, Phil reflected that he and Jill had broken up because, as much as they cared about each other, they could not resolve certain differences in lifestyle and beliefs. He then inwardly rejoiced that Jill and Dave were happy and wished them well, whether their relationship lasted a long time or not. This helped him to introduce himself to Dave, and the two men chatted about sports for some time. While doing so, in his mind Phil continued to rejoice not only in Dave's and Jill's happiness, but also in the happiness of all harmonious couples. After leaving the market, Phil sat in his car and relished the good feeling in his heart. He was astounded by his ability to let go of antipathy and transform the situation.

The great sages say that rejoicing in others' virtue is the lazy person's way to create positive potential and to have a happy mind. Why? Because without having to do the wonderful deeds ourselves, we simply allow ourselves to be happy when others do them. Of course, this is no excuse for not putting forth energy ourselves. We should contribute to the well-being of the world, and by making us admire what is constructive, rejoicing increases our tendency to do that.

People's attention so often goes to what is wrong that they fall into despair. Bombarded by the news, which primarily reports conflicts and catastrophes, they forget the continual kindness that people show each other. The rejoicing meditation is an antidote to this. It is easy to do and can be done anywhere. For example, while standing in line at the bank, we can rejoice in the wealth—no matter how great—that others have, and at the same time pray that wealth increase and be more equally distributed. While waiting at the dentist's office, we can rejoice in the kindness of all dentists and in the help people receive from them, while also praying that everyone with dental problems has access to the help he needs. Upon hearing someone receiving an award for excellence, we can be pleased with their talent and others' recognition of it. When our colleagues leave on vacation, we can rejoice that they will have the opportunity to relax and enjoy themselves. Similarly, we can applaud those who are more disciplined than we are in their daily meditation practice. We can be happy at others' generosity, whether or not we are the recipient of it, and we can appreciate others' patience, tolerance, and open-mindedness in situations that we would find difficult. When someone solves a problem that we cannot, we can celebrate her knowledge and skill, and when we see others' happiness, we can be delighted.

When attentive, we will find more situations each day in which we can practice rejoicing. By each day making a mental note of our pleasure in others' good fortune, well-being, virtue, and excellent qualities, we will become joyful. In addition, this positive mental attitude will transform our speech and actions, so that we praise others and celebrate them. This, in turn, will transform our relationships with those with whom we are in daily contact. In addition, our mindstream will be enriched by a wealth of positive potential, which will enhance our spiritual practice and facilitate our realizing the steps of the path. All in all, only good, no harm, will come from abandoning envy and instead rejoicing.

Chapter Fifteen

ANGER AT OURSELVES

Sometimes we become angry with ourselves, blaming ourselves for being incompetent or unlovable. This often leads to depression and more self-hatred. While recognizing our mistakes and weaknesses is wise, we needn't hate ourselves for having them. We are sentient beings—just like everyone else—caught in cyclic existence due to our disturbing attitudes, negative emotions, and karma. Of course we aren't perfect. We have foibles, but we do not need to identify with them so strongly. They are not our identity; they are not an inherent part of ourselves. By reflecting in this way, we can become more patient with ourselves and still be motivated to change.

Have Love and Compassion for Ourselves

Love is the wish that sentient beings have happiness and its causes and compassion is the wish that they be free from suffering and its causes. Since we, too, are sentient beings, our love and compassion must encompass ourselves as well as others. The Tibetan words which are translated as love and compassion, unlike the English words themselves, imply having these sentiments towards ourselves as well as others.

However, many people confuse loving themselves with being selfish. This error manifests in two quite different ways. Some people, thinking selfishness is bad and wanting to avoid it, also stop loving themselves. They have a low opinion of themselves, feel guilty if they are too happy, and deny themselves pleasures. From a Buddhist viewpoint, low self-esteem and this type of self-denial are as caught up with self-centeredness as pride is, for they all over-estimate the importance of the self and focus on it in an unhealthy way.

Other people, thinking loving themselves is good, fall to the extreme of self-indulgence and selfishness. To show their love for themselves, they say, for example, "I'm going to buy myself a present." When our coat is torn, we may need to buy ourselves a new coat. This is not self-indulgent. However, sometimes "buying ourselves a present" is permeated with self-centeredness: "*I* want this expensive coat so that *I* will feel good." In this instance, we are no longer just taking care of ourselves but are being self-indulgent. Activities done with this attitude do not really make us happy, because our mind is focused on only our own immediate pleasure.

How then do we correctly differentiate self-love from selfishness? Selfishness in Buddhism means self-centeredness and self-preoccupation—that is, thinking of ourselves first and foremost. Whether we think of ourselves as the worst of all or the best of all, we are nonetheless exaggerating the importance of the self. Both self-hatred and self-indulgence are extremes. Neither brings happiness or eliminates misery. We are one among countless sentient beings, all of whom want to be happy and to avoid suffering as intensely as we do. We are neither more important nor less important than others. Thus, in wishing all beings to be happy and free from suffering, we must include ourselves. Doing so is appropriately loving ourselves and having compassion for ourselves. No sentient being is more or less deserving than any other in this respect.

Focus on the Positive

When we are angry at ourselves, we frequently see only what is flawed in our lives. This view is extremely narrow and is comparable to focusing on the one spot on a table while ignoring the beauty of the whole table. Joseph purchased some land to build a holiday cabin. For days he carefully laid the bricks for one of the walls, a difficult job because positioning the bricks neatly on top of each other required skill that he was still developing. Surveying the completed work, he saw two crooked bricks and berated himself for making such an unsightly wall.

Later that afternoon, his friend Larry stopped by and commented, "What a fantastic wall you made!"

"But don't you see the two crooked bricks?" asked Joseph. "They ruined the whole thing."

"Yes, I see them," responded Larry, "but I also see the hundreds of beautifully arranged ones that make the wall pleasing to the eye."

Value Our Good Circumstances

We often focus on a few circumstances in our life that aren't going well instead of all those that are. Although we all have problems, when we over-emphasize their importance, we easily begin thinking that we are incapable and worthless. Such self-hatred immobilizes us and prevents us from developing our good qualities and sharing them with others.

When we look at the broad picture, however, we can see many positive things in our life. We can rejoice that we are alive and appreciate whatever degree of good health we have. We also have food (often too much!), shelter, clothing, medicine, friends, relatives, and a myriad of good circumstances. Many of the people reading this book live in peaceful places, not in war-torn areas. Many have jobs they like, and family and friends they appreciate. We shouldn't take these for granted. Most importantly, from a spiritual viewpoint, we have access to an authentic path, qualified teachers to guide us, and kind companions who encourage us. We have genuine spiritual aspirations and the time to cultivate these. Thinking about these good conditions one by one, we will be filled with joy, and any sense of being incapable and hopeless will vanish.

Acknowledge Our Mistakes and Laugh at Ourselves

We frequently respond to our mistakes with guilt and don't want anyone else to know what we did. However, acknowledging our errors is psychologically and spiritually healthy and prevents our developing the internal heaviness that comes with shame. Due to this honesty, self-confidence will arise and we no longer will fear others knowing our mistakes. As we make amends for our blunders, we can also begin to have a sense of humor about them.

Ellen, the competent manager of a real estate firm, cultivated precision and accountability in her staff. When the photographs of an important client's property were missing, she asked everyone to look in their folders and workspaces. When they were still nowhere to be found, she assembled the staff and gave them a stern lecture about responsibility and consideration for others. She hoped that someone would acknowledge misplacing them, but no one did. Frustrated and angry, she returned to her desk, contemplating how to explain this to the client. However, when she opened her briefcase to get his telephone number, there were the photos in an envelope addressed to her; she had hurriedly put them there while rushing to a meeting the previous week. She broke out laughing and, waving the envelope in her hand, told the staff of her mistake. They accepted her apology and laughed with her as she acknowledged her own error.

Accept Ourselves as We Are

Indicating how harshly we criticize ourselves, someone once said, "If we treated others the way we treat ourselves, we wouldn't have any friends." In fact, sometimes we mentally flog ourselves for our weaknesses and mistakes. This is useless and, in fact, is an impediment to spiritual progress. How then can we view our foibles?

With self-acceptance, we can let go of judgment and acknowledge what we are or have done. Looking back at the person we were when we erred, we can understand and have compassion for her suffering. At that time, we did what we thought was best. Confusion clouded our mind, and we erred. Although we need to make amends for the harm we inflicted on others, we need not hate and condemn ourselves. We can forgive ourselves. While the action was mistaken, the person who did it was not evil.

Remember Our Buddha Potential

On the deepest level, the nature of our mind is untainted. The cloud-like destructive emotions can be eliminated. In addition, we have the seeds of all enlightened qualities in our mindstream, and these can be developed limitlessly, until we attain full enlightenment. This Buddha nature is an innate part of our mind and is always present.

The prisoners with whom I correspond have committed atrocious acts. When they tell me about them, they inevitably add, "I hope that you won't think I'm despicable and that you will continue to write to me." Knowing they have the potential to become fully enlightened beings, I reassure them of my commitment. My faith in their Buddha potential helps them to see this quality in themselves. When they do this, they begin to bloom, acknowledging their mistakes, correcting their wrong attitudes, and re-directing their energies in a positive way.

Accepting that the nature of our mind/heart is pure can be challenging. When he encountered the Dharma, Philip was serving a long sentence for rape and assault. Studying and practicing for months, he requested his spiritual advisor, a Buddhist nun, to do the refuge ceremony during which he would formally commit himself to the Buddhist path. At the conclusion of the ceremony, she gave him the Buddhist name, Gunaratna, "The Essence of the Gem of Virtue." He laughed and said, "C'mon, 'The Essence of the Gem of Virtue?' That's not me. You must be thinking of someone else! Don't you know what I've done?"

She replied, "Gunaratna, stop it! That man doesn't exist any more. Virtue is the ideal you will embrace and actualize in this life." Her direct and matter-of-fact reply, filled with tough love, overwhelmed him. He then began to have faith in his untainted nature and that has given him tremendous inspiration to change. Now he says, "I want to think, feel, and act in the best interest of others," and he has undertaken to do that even though he is living in a violent and rough prison.

Aspire to Change

Wishing ourselves to be free from suffering and to have happiness, we aspire to change in order to bring this about. Such love and compassion for ourselves is part of our motivation to become a better welder, musician, or parent and to practice the path to enlightenment.

Having the determination to be free from the suffering of cyclic existence is compassion for ourselves. In addition, having the wish to become a Buddha in order to benefit all beings includes wishing ourselves to have the highest happiness, that of full enlightenment. This wish, however, is not based on self-centeredness, but on care and respect for all beings. Appreciating our potential and aspiring to develop it are important. We can feel joyful that the path to enlightenment exists and that we have the capability to practice it.

Purify Negativities

When we make mistakes, rather than wallowing in guilt, we benefit from purifying them and continuing on the path. The Buddha prescribed a four-step process for doing this. First, we review our actions and genuinely regret those that harmed others or ourselves. Such actions are inevitably motivated by ignorance, anger, or attachment. Regret differs from guilt. Based on a balanced view of the self, regret arises from accurately assessing our actions. Guilt, on the other hand, is a form of self-hatred. Based on a negative view of the self, it arises from over-emphasizing the negativity of our mistakes. By regretting our errors, we can learn from them and improve in the future, whereas by feeling guilty, we remain locked in an unproductive downward spiral.

Second, regret leads us to determine not to act destructively again. While we can confidently say we will abandon some harmful actions forever, we may know that we are not yet able to avoid others completely. In those cases, we can set ourselves a reasonable period of time during which we will be especially mindful and not engage in those actions. In this way, we will gradually become confident in our ability to develop positive habits.

Third, we make amends to those whom we have harmed or towards whom we have had negative attitudes or feelings. In the case of other sentient beings, we develop love, compassion, and the altruistic intention to attain enlightenment for the benefit of all. This counteracts the force of our previous negative intentions towards them. In the case of religious figures and refuge objects, we recall their good qualities and generate faith and trust in them.

The best way of making amends is through transforming our attitude, letting go of any hostility or other destructive emotion we may still harbor towards another person. In addition, it is to our advantage to overcome our pride or shame and directly apologize to the person we harmed and compensate her for any physical damage we have done. Nevertheless, this is not essential, for sometimes the other person has already passed away or does not wish to receive communication or help from us.

Fourth, to "walk the talk," we engage in some sort of remedial action. This includes such activities as community service, volunteer work, service work, meditation, or religious practice, such as bowing, reciting prayers and mantras, and meditating.

Many Buddhists engage in these four opponent powers on a daily basis. In this way, they avoid stockpiling any negative feelings or karmic imprints over time. Psychologically healthy, as well as spiritually beneficial, regularly purifying our mistakes lays the foundation for a happy mind, which, in turn, reduces the likelihood of anger arising within us. By developing and cleansing our minds through Dharma practice, we can become Buddhas. Hating ourselves is hating a Buddha-to-be, which is certainly inappropriate!

Chapter Sixteen

CULTIVATING LOVE AND COMPASSION

> While the enemy—your own anger—is unsubdued,
> Though you conquer external foes, they will only increase.
> Therefore with the militia of love and compassion
> Subdue your own mind—
> This is the practice of bodhisattvas.
> —Gyalsey Togme Sangpo in
> *The Thirty-seven Practices of Bodhisattvas*

In the preceding chapters, we examined various situations in which our anger tends to arise and the antidotes to bring our mind to a more balanced state. In this chapter, we will explore particularly potent medicine to counter and prevent anger: love and compassion. Love is the wish for beings to have happiness and its causes; compassion is the wish for them to be free from suffering and its causes. Anger, on the other hand, wishes to inflict harm. Thus love and compassion are diametrically opposed to anger. For this reason, love and compassion are effective in both counteracting and preventing anger.

See the Advantages of a Kind Heart

In *The Precious Garland*, the Indian sage Nagarjuna spoke of several advantages of being loving and compassionate. Among these are that others will not harm us, but will be friendly and protect us; our mind will be happy and free of stress, and thus our body will be healthier as well; and attaining our aims will be facilitated. Also, we will die peacefully, and after death we will have a good rebirth and progress along the path to enlightenment.

However, we cannot simply wish our love and compassion into existence. As with any other positive mental habit, we must cultivate these over time. Since causes definitely bring their results, if we continuously train our minds in love and compassion, eventually these emotions will arise spontaneously and effortlessly within us.

The Buddha spoke of two main methods to cultivate love, compassion, and altruism. They are called the seven cause and effect instructions, and equalizing and exchanging self and others. These have been described in depth in many books. One of my teachers, Geshe Jampa Tegchok, explained these especially lucidly in his book *Transforming the Heart: The Buddhist Way to Joy and Courage*. Here, I will explain some simple activities we can do to develop love and compassion.

Meditate on the Kindness of Others

Before we can wish sentient beings well, we have to see them as lovable, and to do that, we remember their kindness towards us. Here kindness does not mean that others necessarily had the conscious intention to benefit us, but simply that we have benefited from their actions. In this meditation, we begin by recalling the help, support, and encouragement we have received from family and friends. Thinking of specific people and particular acts of kindness is very effective. However, in recalling these, we do not let attachment arise for our dear ones, but simply feel a sense of gratitude, whereby we do not take others for granted but appreciate what they have done and continue to do for us.

Then, we consider the benefit we have received from parents, relatives, and teachers. They have cared for us as best they could. When we were young, they protected us from danger and gave us an education. They taught us to speak, read, and write, as well as how to get along with others. All of our talents, abilities, and skills are due to the people who taught and trained us. Without their interest and encouragement, we would never have gained knowledge or developed our unique talents.

In addition, we consider the kindness of strangers. They have grown our food, made our clothes, and constructed our homes and workplaces. They have worked in mines and factories to build the cars, computers, and appliances that we use. Although we do not know these people personally, without them we could not remain alive, nor could we enjoy all the things we currently use. When we become familiar with this step in the meditation, we cease to be annoyed with construction work on the highways but instead consider the kindness of the people who improve the roads for us. We are automatically more polite and cheerful to airline employees, civil servants, salespeople, and those in bureaucratic positions. Our new appreciation of employees at the gas station, supermarket, and bank is reflected in how we interact with them, and this enriches their lives as well as ours.

Finally, we consider the benefit we have received from people with whom we don't get along and from those who have harmed us. Although superficially they seem to harm and not help us, in fact, we learn a great deal from them. They point out our weaknesses so that we can remedy them. They challenge us to go beyond what is comfortable and secure for our self-centered ego and to grow in ways that we otherwise never would have. In addition, these people give us the chance to develop patience, tolerance, and compassion, qualities that are essential for evolving spiritually. We can feel grateful to them for this.

Having considered the benefit we receive from each of the above groups, we then let our mind rest in the feeling of gratitude. Rather than feeling that the world and those in it are uncaring, we realize that we have been the recipient of incalculable benefit throughout our lives. Feeling this, our mind is happy, and the wish to be kind in return naturally arises within us.

Meditation on Love

Remembering that love is the wish for sentient beings to have happiness and its causes, we begin by reflecting on the meaning of happiness. Two types of happiness exist, temporal and supreme. Temporal happiness is experienced while we are still in cyclic existence. It includes having food, clothing, shelter, medicine, friends, pleasures from objects of the senses, good reputation, and so forth. Supreme happiness comes from internal transformation, cleansing our mind of defilements, such as ignorance and self-centeredness, and enhancing its good qualities, such as compassion and wisdom. This is the happiness we experience when we have stable spiritual realizations. It is the bliss of liberation and enlightenment. Thus, when we go through each category of people in the meditation, we wish them both temporal happiness and its causes—positive actions—and supreme happiness and its causes.

We begin by wishing ourselves to be well and happy, not in a selfish way, but in a way that respects and cares for ourself as one of many sentient beings. Then, we gradually spread this well-wishing to friends and family. We think, feel, and imagine, "May my friends and all those who have been kind to me have happiness and its causes. May they be free from suffering, confusion, and fear. May they have calm, peaceful, and fulfilled hearts." To conclude, we rest our mind in this feeling.

Next, we generate the same feeling for people we don't know—all those whose work in society contributes to our happiness.

When this is stable, we wish all those who have harmed us, those whom we fear or feel threatened by, and those of whom we disapprove to have happiness and its causes. At first our mind may be resistant to this due to longtime habits of resentment and hostility. But if we remember that these people have acted in ways to which we object because they have been in pain or confused, then we see that wishing them to be happy is wishing for the causes of their harmful behavior to be alleviated. This does not mean that we wish an alcoholic to have an ample supply of liquor. Rather we wish him to have a peaceful mind and self-confidence, so that he no longer sees alcohol as a way to deal with his pain.

Finally, we spread this loving feeling to all sentient beings, including animals and insects. Having done this, we rest our mind one-pointedly in the feeling of love, so that it becomes ingrained and familiar to us.

Understand Compassion

Compassion is the wish for sentient beings to be free from suffering and its causes. His Holiness the Dalai Lama constantly speaks of the advantages and necessity of a kind heart and compassion. In fact, he counsels, "If you can cherish others more than yourself, good. But if you want to be selfish, at least be wisely selfish, and that means to take care of others." Here he is emphasizing our interdependence as sentient beings and our need to support each other for the well-being of all. If we care simply for ourselves and disregard others, our well-being will be threatened, because it depends on others. If we live surrounded by others who are deprived or unhappy, we will be affected by witnessing the pain of their circumstances. In addition, our own comfortable circumstances may be disrupted as they, in their struggle for happiness, resort to activities that we find distasteful, harmful, or threatening. This is true within families, groups and nations, and on the international level. If we could arrange for those who are unhappy to find happiness by more productive means, they would surely do so. Therefore, for the sake of even our own happiness, we must help others.

Several years ago, the citizens in Seattle were voting on a school bond. Some people who did not have school-aged children said, "Why should our property taxes be used to educate others' children?" Some of these same people, however, were happy for their taxes to be used to build more prisons in the state. I found this logic baffling. If children have a good education and enjoyable activities in which to engage during and after school, they are more likely to become good citizens and not resort to crime. Well-balanced children, no matter whose children they are, influence society positively. Similarly, children deprived of education and love, no matter whose children they are, are more likely to harm others. Since we all live in the same environment, it serves our own selfish interests, as well as the interests of others, to see that poverty, lack of education, and job discrimination are eliminated.

Westerners often misunderstand compassion. Some people think that it lays the groundwork for others to take advantage of us. They reason that if we are kind and forgiving, others will treat us unfairly. However, the wish for others to be free of suffering is not a foolhardy, idealistic notion. It is an attitude that opens and calms our mind so that our decisions are based on wisdom. Compassion does not mean doing everything everyone else wants. Rather, compassion supported by wisdom is assertive and precise.

Some believe that to be truly compassionate, we must suffer ourselves. Therefore, they are reluctant to be compassionate. However, from the Buddhist viewpoint, compassion can come only from a happy mind. If we feel we must sacrifice ourselves and fear the misery of doing so, our mind cannot become genuinely generous. Therefore, we must have love and compassion also for ourselves and care for ourselves, not out of selfishness, but because we, too, are sentient beings who want happiness and freedom from suffering. Deeply caring for ourselves includes counteracting mental attitudes that make us miserable, including self-neglect and self-negation. As we do this, our ability to be generous and compassionate will increase.

In recent years, I have traveled to Israel to teach meditation and share Buddhist perspectives. During those trips, I also visited the West Bank and the Gaza Strip, the site of the future Palestine. While I was writing this book in Seattle in the autumn of 2000, horrible violence erupted in the Middle East. The meditation groups in Tel Aviv and Jerusalem phoned me on a conference call to request a "telephone-teaching." "How can we prevent our minds from hardening in reaction to this violence? How can we be compassionate towards those who blow up buses filled with innocent children? How do we protect ourselves from the negative energy of those around us, be they Israelis or Palestinians?" they asked. These are hard questions and remind us that the discussion of compassion is not theoretical and idealistic, but deeply practical. It is relevant to our lives.

Israelis are not strangers to suffering. The parents of many of those who called me were Holocaust survivors or refugees from other countries. I asked them to look at the Palestinians as they look at their own people. "Think of what the Palestinians feel. Imagine you were born and raised in a refugee camp. Around you, you saw wealthier and more powerful people. You heard your family's stories of being displaced from your home, and you feel your family's pain as they struggle to make a living amidst high unemployment and job discrimination." Then I asked, "Do you get a sense of how they see the world? Although rage on anyone's part brings harm, can you understand how they may feel this? If you, too, succumb to rage, how will that affect you?"

I spoke about the meaning and the necessity of compassion, "You can be compassionate and simultaneously condemn harmful behavior. Israelis and Palestinians are mixed geographically and interdependent economically and politically. The Palestinians aren't leaving the area and neither are the Israelis. So the two peoples will have to find a way to live together, because the alternative for your children is too horrible to contemplate. For this to happen, you must have the courage to cultivate compassion over a long time, no matter what happens."

Meditate on Compassion

When meditating to develop compassion, we wish ourselves and all others to be free from physical, mental, and emotional suffering, as well as its causes—disturbing attitudes, negative emotions, and karma. As with the meditation on love, we begin by focusing on ourselves and thinking, "May I be free from physical, mental, and emotional suffering. May fear, anger, and aggression not afflict me. May I be free from craving and dissatisfaction, and may stupidity, confusion, and ignorance plague me no more. May I be free from apathy, jealousy, and pride." We feel this wish deeply and imagine ourselves being free from these.

As in the above meditations, we gradually expand this feeling first to friends and family, then to strangers, then to those whom we distrust or who have harmed us, and finally to all sentient beings. At the conclusion, we let our mind abide single-pointedly in this feeling of compassion and be saturated by it.

Meditate on Taking and Giving

The Indian sage Dharmaraksita advised in *The Wheel of Sharp Weapons*:

> As all that is wrong can be traced to one source,
> Our concern for ourselves whom we cherish the most,
> We must meditate now on the kindness of others.
> Accepting the suffering that they never wished for,
> We must dedicate fully our virtues to all.

> Thus taking upon ourselves all deluded non-virtuous
>   actions
> That others have done in the past, present, and future,
> With mind, speech, and body,
> May disturbing emotions of others as well as our own
> Be the favored conditions to gain our enlightenment,
> Just as peacocks eat poison to thrive.

These verses describe the taking and giving meditation, a method to transform our suffering and disturbing emotions into the path to enlightenment. Just as peacocks, by eating the poison of certain plants, thrive and produce their beautiful fans, so we can use others' suffering and our own disturbing emotions to produce love, compassion, and wisdom, and consequently enlightenment.

Thus, we do the taking and giving meditation to enhance and strengthen our love and compassion. Normally we wish to have all pleasure, success, and good opportunities ourselves and shun any disadvantages, pain, or suffering. As explained in previous chapters, this self-centered attitude keeps us bound in dissatisfaction, makes us insensitive to others, and ignores the harmful influence our negative actions have on them. In this meditation, we recall that the self-centered attitude is our real enemy. We then generate strong compassion that wishes to take on others' suffering and strong love that wishes to give them our happiness. Although we cannot actually take others' illness from them and give them our good health, for example, just developing the wish to be able to do so and imagining doing so purifies our mind and increases our ability to directly help others in the future.

Geshe Tegchok's book gives elaborate instructions on the taking and giving meditation. In brief, we begin by imagining in front of us one or more people who are suffering and generate compassion for them. When this compassion is strong, we imagine their suffering and its causes flowing out from them in the form of pollution and black smoke, which we then inhale. However, we do not sit there with this inside us, but instead transform it into a thunderbolt, which then smashes and completely obliterates the lump at our heart of our own self-centeredness, ignorance, anger, and attachment. We rest in the open space at our heart and experience the peaceful absence of wrong conceptions and self-centeredness.

Within this space, we cultivate love for those same people and imagine white light radiating from our heart to them. We imagine transforming our body, possessions, and positive potential into everything they need for temporal and supreme happiness. We then increase all these and send them out to the people envisioned before us. We imagine them being satisfied and happy and even attaining the ultimate joy of enlightenment. To conclude, we rejoice that we were able effect this. Although this is done on the level of imagination, it can have a powerful effect on ourselves and others.

The taking and giving meditation is an excellent antidote to deal with specific problems. We can imagine others with the same difficulty from which we are suffering and think, "As long as I am experiencing misery due to this problem, may it suffice for all others who are similarly suffering." In other words, we think, "By my enduring this, which I must do in any case, may others be free from pain." We envision before us people we know or about whom we have read who are experiencing the particular difficulty. We take this problem from them and use it to destroy the negative emotions inside us. As we give our body, possessions, and positive potential to others, we imagine that their minds become loving and peaceful.

After her parents' sudden death. Jessica felt grief mixed with anger and a sense of injustice. Using the taking and giving meditation to help her process these emotions, she imagined all the people who had experienced sudden loss in front of her. Developing compassion for the various confused emotions they felt, she thought, "May my sorrow and anger suffice for their suffering" and visualized taking on their disturbing emotions in the form of pollution. As she inhaled the pollution, it turned into a thunderbolt which destroyed the lump of grief and fury at her heart. She let her mind relax in that empty space, free from conceptions about who she was or what had happened. Then from her heart, white light radiated to all those people. She imagined transforming her body, possessions, and positive potential into the objects and companions they needed, then multiplying these, and sending them out to the people. When they received them, their sufferings were pacified, they turned their minds to the Dharma, and through practice, they attained enlightenment. Then, Jessica rested her mind in joy that this had occurred. When she got up from her meditation session, her own mind was calm, and the previous sense of overwhelming loss had subsided.

Similarly, in conjunction with therapy, Dorothy used the taking and giving meditation as an antidote to her resentment caused by the breakup of her marriage. Bruce did it to calm his rage at racial prejudice directed against him, and Margaret used it to counteract bitterness due to misogyny she had encountered. Martin did this meditation to cope with his pain caused by cancer. In all these cases, by putting their own happiness and suffering into perspective and developing genuine love and compassion for others, these individuals were able to transform their negative experiences, and render their minds peaceful. They discovered that the internal happiness gained through developing a kind heart is supreme to all other types of happiness.

Practice Visualization and Chanting Meditations

Tibetan Buddhism is rich with visualization practices that pacify anger and develop love and compassion. Some of these may be adapted for use by those of any faith as well as the non-religious. For example, in one meditation we imagine feeling impartial love and compassion for each and every living being. We then visualize this love and compassion appearing as a ball of light in the space in front of us. Light flows into us from this radiant sphere, purifying all our anger, hurt, and bitterness. This brilliant light fills our body completely, permeating our entire nervous system and making both our body and mind calm and blissful. We concentrate on feeling free from all disturbing emotions. After a while, we imagine light again flowing from the radiant sphere into us, this time filling us with patience, love, compassion, and all the good qualities we wish to develop. We focus on feeling that we have generated these positive qualities and can express them easily and appropriately in our daily interactions with others. At the conclusion of the meditation, we imagine the radiant sphere, which is the essence of all good qualities, coming to the top of our head and dissolving into us. It comes to rest at our heart center, in the center of our chest, and we feel that our heart/mind has become inseparable from this love and compassion.

In another meditation, we recite the mantra of Avalokiteshvara, the Buddha of Compassion, who is also known as Chenresig in Tibetan, Kuan Yin in Chinese, and Kannon in Japanese. The mantra *om mani padme hum*—Tibetans pronounce it *om mani pey may hum*—roughly means "the jewel in the lotus." "Jewel" refers to the compassionate aspect of the path to enlightenment, while "lotus" refers to the wisdom aspect. Just as a bird needs two wings to fly, we need to develop both of these qualities in order to become a fully enlightened being.

Reciting the mantra repeatedly, either quickly or slowly, out loud or silently, helps us to focus our attention in a positive way. This is especially effective when our mind is ruminating with unproductive thoughts or disturbing emotions. Simply centering our mind on the soothing syllables said by an enlightened being alleviates our anger and misery. Some people like to recite the mantra and at the same time, imagine being filled with loving light, as in the visualization described above.

Practice Love and Compassion in Our Lives

His Holiness the Dalai Lama often says, "My religion is kindness." In saying this, he emphasizes that kindness is the essence of all religions and instructs us to make kindness the center of our life. We can do this in many ways. First, in the morning when we awake, we can generate a kind motivation: "Today as much as possible I will not harm anyone, and as much as possible I will help others." Then, throughout the day, we should be mindful of this motivation and act from it.

We do not need to be a great being such as Mother Theresa in order to help others. Rather, we should help whomever we meet however we can in whatever situation we are. This can include being cheerful at breakfast with our family each morning, smiling at a colleague who is gloomy, greeting the clerk at the supermarket, and being courteous to those who help us when we call airlines, government offices, and large companies. Instead of seeing others as beings whose duty it is to please us, we should be friendly and recognize that a small act of kindness can make a big difference in their day.

In addition, according to our resources, we can give to charities that benefit the sick, hungry, and poor, and those challenged in various ways. Similarly, we can do volunteer work at community service jobs, such as tutoring children, leading nature hikes, finding homes for stray animals, and doing hospice work for the dying. In essence, by sharing our kind heart with everyone whom we encounter, we will use our lives to solve more problems than we create.

Chapter Seventeen

HELPING OTHERS SUBDUE THEIR ANGER

We know from our own experiences how painful and damaging anger can be. When people we care about—family, friends, and colleagues—are agitated, defensive, or resentful, we see their suffering and wish to help. How can we do this?

Listen to Friends Who Are Angry

When someone asks me, "How do I help a friend who is angry?" I usually begin by asking her first to look at her own anger, for all too often, we try to solve someone else's problem with anger without acknowledging our own. When we say we want to help a friend who is fuming, we really mean, "That person is angry at me, and I don't like that. How can I get him to change?" In such cases we need to be directed back to the introspective process of dealing with our own hostility and establishing our own inner calm.

Sometimes, however, the other's upset is not directed at us, and seeing him suffer, we want to help. Skill is needed, for we need to be sensitive to each situation. One stock response will not work at all times. Very often, listening with our heart is the best medicine. Here, we let our friend explain the events and her feelings without interrupting to offer advice. When she pauses for a while, we may let her know we understood by summarizing the content of what she said or labeling the feelings she was expressing.

It is never helpful to tell someone that what he is feeling is wrong or that he should not feel that way. Similarly, jumping in and trying to fix the situation often leaves our friend feeling misunderstood. He wasn't looking for a solution; he simply wanted to be heard. Wanting to fix the situation is often indicative of our own discomfort with someone's emotions. In this case, we need to look inside ourselves, recognize what we are feeling and why, and apply appropriate antidotes.

Do Not Take Sides

Helping a friend who is irate does not mean taking her side in an argument against another. This only adds fuel to the fire and reinforces, not reduces, her anger. A real friend is one who assists the other person in examining and calming her emotions. Thus, to help our friends when they are upset, we should listen with acceptance, ask questions, and offer observations that will help them to reflect on the situation in a different way.

Marilyn had just had an argument with Cori during lunch time at their college. After school, she called her friend Anne. Complaining vehemently about Cori, Marilyn tried to get Anne to take part in a scheme to get back at her. Anne refused. Instead, she said to Marilyn, "You sound pretty upset. What is *really* bothering you?" After some time, with gentle coaching, Marilyn was able to admit to being jealous of Cori. Anne helped her to stop comparing herself to Cori and to focus on her own talents and qualities. In this way, she genuinely helped her friend and prevented further quarrels and backbiting from occurring.

Let Go When We Cannot Help

It may happen that whatever support we try to give, our friends or relatives remain stuck in their anger. At such times, we may feel frustrated and start to become angry with them for not accepting our help or following our advice. Clearly, this compounds the problem, for now not only are they angry, but so are we!

When our attempts to help have not brought the desired outcome, we must accept the situation. Often we cannot control our own mind, let alone someone else's! We should cease to offer advice, but keep our heart open to the other person. We may discover later that some of what we said had an effect.

Marvin, a man in his eighties, began to use a wheel chair after surgery a few years ago. Because he complained of discomfort from sitting in his wheelchair, his children offered to get him a better one. He angrily refused their generosity, insisting that he would walk again soon, even though he had not put much effort into regaining his strength. His neighbor Ethyl knew that trying to convince him to get a new wheelchair was useless, but she was concerned about the effect his anger was having on his relationship with his family. She tried to help him acknowledge and let go of his anger, but Marvin's attitude wouldn't shift. She then backed off discussing this topic while continuing her friendship with him. While they were playing cards a few weeks later, Marvin turned to her and said, "Ethyl, you were right about my being unreasonably angry at my children. Although I still don't want a new wheelchair, I do want to love my children and receive their love. I'm stopping my part in this feud." Marvin did, and his children reciprocated.

Sometimes I find it helpful to ask a friend who is at an impasse, "What could someone say that would help you at this moment?" This sometimes helps him to consider new alternatives. Similarly, if a friend is still ruminating on an event from years ago, I may ask, "What could someone have said to you back then that would have helped you?" Often this stimulates the person to look at the situation more creatively.

Teach Children to Work with Their Anger

My sister called me recently, perplexed about how to handle my three-year-old nephew's outbursts of anger. "He's not afraid of anything," she said. "If I shout at him, he gets angrier. If I threaten him with going to his room for a time-out, he just screams louder."

I remembered the times when, as a child, I didn't get what I wanted and was angry. Unlike my nephew, an adult yelling at me often intimidated me into being quiet. However, rather than subduing my anger, I generally became angrier although I didn't express it. Similarly, when I was punished for quarreling with my siblings, the outward quarrel stopped, but my anger didn't. Now, hearing of my nephew's difficulty, I wondered what would have helped me work with my anger when I was a child

"Try not to threaten him with punishment," I suggested to my sister. "See if you can help him put into words what is bothering him. He needs to learn how to work with his anger, not to be punished for having it. He's still young so you'll need to help him find the words to fit his experience, but as he grows older, being able to identify his feelings and the external conditions that provoke them will help him."

I went on to tell her that as an adult, I voluntarily take a time-out when I'm upset. For me, a time-out is not a punishment, but an opportunity to calm down and let go of my unhappiness. Then, when the heat of the anger has passed, I can look at and deal with the situation more clearly. If we can convey this same attitude about a time-out to our children, they will learn to regulate themselves and take a time-out when they need it, without feeling that they are being punished for being upset.

Be a Good Example

Children learn by observing their parents. If parents can identify their anger, apply antidotes to subdue it, and apologize when they make an antagonist remark, their children will copy their example. Thus, as often happens, children become good mirrors for parents to review their own attitudes and behaviors. When parents love their children and want the best for them, they are more motivated to work with their anger and develop a kind heart so that they can be a good example for their children.

In recent years, some educators and psychologists have developed effective means to aid children in identifying their emotions and working with them. For more information on this subject, I refer you to the work of Dr. Mark Greenberg from Pennsylvania State University and the PATHS (Promoting Alternative Thinking Strategies) curriculum he developed.

Love Children When They're Angry

Miriam, now in her eighties, told me a moving story of how her parents dealt with her anger. At ages three and six, she had made a child's short-lived attempt to run away from home when she was unhappy with her parents' not giving into her whims. At age nine, she was again mad at them and wanted to leave. But she had learned a lesson from the two previous attempts and knew she needed provisions. Going into the kitchen, she said to her mother, "I want an apple, a banana, and a sandwich."

"Why?" her mother asked.

"I'm going to run away from home," Miriam retorted.

"Oh, don't do that," her mother replied gently. "I love you and will miss you terribly." Miriam began to cry and rushed to hug her mother, who embraced her lovingly.

How many of us get angry when we are really trying to say "please love me"? And how many of us miss others' pleas for kindness because we react to their outer hostility?

Chapter Eighteen

WISDOM THAT RELAXES THE MIND

The Buddha's teaching speaks of two principal types of wisdom. The first understands karma and its effects and knows the functioning of phenomena in the relative world. The second realizes the deeper mode of existence, that all phenomena and persons lack independent or inherent existence. Both of these types of wisdom aid in the cessation of unhappiness that produces anger, but the latter especially relaxes our mind by cutting all false projections. For that reason, we will now discuss how to use it to counteract and eventually eliminate anger and other painful, disturbing emotions.

As noted previously, anger and other destructive emotions are based on false projections of the mind. While the inappropriate attention that nourishes anger projects or exaggerates negative qualities, our ignorance projects an even deeper distortion: independent or inherent existence. While at one level we know that things exist dependently—sprouts grow from seeds, a table depends on its parts—things appear to our mind in the opposite way, as if they had their own essence and existed under their own power, independent from everything else. When we are upset, our "self" or "I" similarly appears to be solid and to exist inherently.

In *The Wheel of Sharp Weapons,* Dharmaraksita states:

> All things are like images found in a mirror,
> And yet we imagine they are real, very real.
> All things are like mist or like clouds on a mountain,
> And yet we imagine they are stable and firm.

> Our foe—our insistence on ego-identities
> Truly our own, which we wish were secure—
> And our butcher—the selfish concern for ourselves—

Like all things these appear to be inherently existent,
Though they never have been inherently existent at all.

Although they appear to be concrete and real,
They have never been real, any time, anywhere.
They are not things we should burden with ultimate value,
Nor should we deny them their relative truth.

Try to Find the "I" That Is Angry

How do we apply this understanding to our daily lives and especially
to situations in which we are vexed or even infuriated? Let's consider,
as an example, a situation in which we are angry because others have
betrayed our trust or been prejudiced against us. Underneath the
anger is hurt, and together with the anger and hurt, we feel a strong
sense of "self"—there is a solid "I" that is hurt and infuriated. We sit
quietly and ask ourselves, "Who is this 'I' that hurts so much?" or
"Who is this 'I' that should be respected and treated better?" In other
words, we try to find the "I," the person that is feeling those strong
emotions. If such a solid, concrete "I" exists, it should be findable
under investigation. We should be able to locate exactly who it is that
feels hurt, that deserves to be treated better, that wants to be respected.

Then, we undertake an investigation of the sort decribed in detail in Buddhist books on wisdom: Am "I" my body? Am "I" my
mind? Am "I" totally separate from my body and mind? When we
analyze deeply, we cannot find this self-sufficient "I." We are left with
only its absence, its non-existence. Abiding in this state of not finding, we experience freedom and peace. There is no solid person who
hurts. There is no independently existing person that has to be defended.
Our mind and heart rest in openness.

Another way to see the non-existence of the solid "I" that feels
hurt is to ask ourselves, "How do I know I'm hurt?" When we investigate, we see that we know this only because the feeling of hurt
exists. Dependent on that feeling, we generate the thought, "I'm
hurt." In other words, because either our body or our mind feels hurt,
we think, "*I* am hurt." Without taking our body and mind into consideration, we would not generate the thought "I." Thus, the "I"
arises dependently. It exists only in relationship to, in dependence

upon, our body and mind. It does not stand on its own. Therefore, it does not exist from its own side, independently. It is empty of being solid or of existing under its own power. Thinking in this way, we arrive at an open state focused on the lack of a concrete "I" who needs to be defended and whose happiness is most important.

Free Ourselves from Anger Completely

From a Buddhist viewpoint, it is possible to eliminate anger and other destructive emotions from our mindstream completely so that they never arise again. How is this achievable? As we have seen, anger misapprehends its objects. It is based on the exaggeration or super-imposition of negative qualities. In addition, it is founded on ignorance, which projects an independent "I" that is unrelated to anything else. Believing in a solid, separate "I," we relate to the world in a self-centered way, considering everything pertaining to ourselves to be the most important.

We can oppose anger on two fronts. First, we familiarize ourselves with love, compassion, and patience, because, being accurate and beneficial emotions, they counteract the self-centeredness that lies behind anger. We can do the meditations to generate these and use them as antidotes to anger. When we are habituated to these positive emotions, they inhibit the arising of anger even in situations where we previously would have been irritated or hostile.

Secondly, we investigate the nature of reality, specifically analyzing the self that is angry. By seeing that the self and all phenomena exist dependently, not independently, we develop the wisdom realizing the emptiness of inherent existence. Familiarizing ourselves with this wisdom through deep and persistent meditation has the power to eliminate ignorance and anger from our mind forever.

It is not an easy job to develop this wisdom which directly perceives emptiness. This realization depends on stable meditative concentration, which in turn depends on living our life with ethical discipline. Directly realizing emptiness also entails purifying our mind of the imprints of our past destructive actions and accumulating a store of positive potential through acting constructively. Thus many other practices are required to lay the foundation for and to support the development of the wisdom realizing reality.

For this reason, we must study and listen to teachings from a qualified spiritual mentor. We must think about these teachings and discuss them with others to ensure that we correctly understand them. Finally, we must put them into practice through meditation, so that our mind becomes thoroughly familiar with them. In that way, our mind is transformed and we progress towards enlightenment or Buddhahood—the state in which all mental defilements have been eliminated and all good qualities have been enhanced to their fullest. Since each of us has the Buddha potential, the basic purity of the mind, enlightenment is a state that each of us can attain if we expend the effort to create the causes for it.

Appendix One

CONFLICT STYLES

In one schema, researchers delineated five categories of conflict style: avoidance, control, accommodation, compromise, and collaboration. While many people tend to use one conflict style more than others, familiarity with each of them gives us versatility, because depending on the specific situation, one style may be more effective than another. From a Buddhist perspective, in every conflict situation, as in all situations, we must check our motivation to see that it is pure. Thus when in a conflict, we should examine two variables: (1) our motivation and (2) the practical effectiveness of various conflict styles for that situation.

With the conflict style of avoidance, we seek to circumvent a conflict by postponing discussion of it, diplomatically changing the topic, withdrawing from the situation, or in some cases denying that conflict exists. This behavior is useful in situations where neither the goal nor the relationship is significant to us and our mind is free from anger or feelings of hopelessness. For example, with a calm mind, Rob ignored his distant cousin's sarcastic remark. Gayle, however, was closer to this cousin and was upset by the remark; but fearing a quarrel, she pretended she didn't hear it. Nevertheless, she vented her anger by gossiping about this cousin to the rest of the family, thus creating more problems for herself and others.

With control, we insist on having our way. In some situations, this style is appropriate, if done with compassion. For example, Ms. McGrane interceded and forcefully broke up a fight between two children on the playground. At other times, when we self-centeredly want to accomplish our goal without caring about the effect on others, control is counter-productive. At meetings, Harvey bulldozed the staff into acting on his proposal by threatening not to participate if they didn't. The staff reluctantly agreed, but because their voices were not taken into consideration during the decision-making process, their work was not well done and arrived late.

With accommodation, we allow or facilitate the accomplishment of the other person's goal or need, sometimes at the expense of our own. As with the other styles, at certain times emphasizing the relationship rather than our goal is appropriate, while at other times it is not. In an example of the former, John wanted to eat Chinese food, but he happily agreed to his wife's wish to eat at an Italian restaurant. Even though they had had Italian food earlier in the week, he took delight in her happiness. In an instance of the latter, a battered woman "forgave" her husband and complied with his manipulative actions.

With compromise, we give in a little on reaching our goal in order to maintain the relationship and let go a little of the closeness of the relationship in order to accomplish our goal. For example, neither Joe nor Julie wanted to sort though the mail or do the laundry. They could have argued over this (control); one could have capitulated to the other (accommodation); or they could have let both the mail and the laundry remain undone (avoidance). However, they compromised and each of them did one task. Before they reached this decision, they checked that both of them were happy with it. They knew that if the compromise was made because one of them felt pressured, the bad feelings generated would later interfere in their relationship.

While we often view compromise as a good solution, in some situations it is not. For example, two teenage sisters quarreled over who would get an orange and decided to split it in half. What they did not realize was that one of them wanted orange juice and the other wanted the orange peel to flavor a cake. They both would have been happier had they discussed their needs. Then one sister would have squeezed the orange for juice and given the peel to the other, and both would have received more than they did by dividing the orange.

Collaboration involves working together to enhance both the relationship and the accomplishment of the goals of each party. While resolving the conflict using this approach may be more time-consuming, it often brings a more lasting resolution. This style is useful, then, in situations where both the relationship and the goal are important to both parties. For example, Murray set up a food bank and Joan established a soup kitchen, but because they were in the same neighborhood, they were competing for volunteers and donations. Realizing this, they decided to join their projects together in mutual support, thus cutting labor and financial costs and enhancing their work.

Like each of the preceding styles, collaboration may be motivated by patience or anger. Murray and Joan relinquished their rivalry and happily collaborated. Two other people, however, could have half-heartedly agreed to the merger out of obligation and later sabotaged the project. In such a case, they should have spent more time clarifying their feelings and discussing the situation.

Conflict styles deal with external behavior. Each style can be done with either a good or bad motivation. In addition, depending on the situation, one style may be more effective than another for resolving a situation. When anger clouds our mind, we lack the mental clarity to choose a conflict style appropriate for the situation. Instead, we tend to react in the same habitual way in all situations. For instance, Jeff reacts aggressively to both an inadvertent comment and a genuine threat. Deborah capitulates on issues when she has valid reasons as well as when she does not. Susan insists on collaborating on everything, at times consuming time that could be better spent on other activities. Using only one conflict style is ineffective and in fact may worsen the situation. A clear and patient mind gives us the opportunity to decide which conflict style to use in a particular situation.

Appendix Two

TECHNIQUES FOR WORKING WITH ANGER IN BRIEF

This brief listing of some of the techniques for working with anger will assist you in recalling and employing them when needed. They are listed according to the chapter in which they are found.

Training in Patience

Mindfully observe our anger
Understand each other's needs and concerns
Ask ourselves whether the other person is happy

Coping with Criticism

Acknowledge our mistakes
Learn from our critics
Deal with false criticism calmly
Communicate well
Leave the situation if necessary
Learn to evaluate ourselves
Allow others their opinions
Don't see criticism where there is none
Counteract the critical, judgmental attitude

The Blaming Game

See how we co-create situations
Look from a broader perspective
Handle illness wisely

When Our Buttons Are Pushed

Know what our buttons are
Close the internal courtroom
Let go of the "rules of the universe"
Discover the real issue

Acceptance and Empowerment

Accept what is happening
Act or relax
Discover power
Have a compassionate heart
Accept that our control is limited

Meeting the Enemy

Give the pain to our self-centeredness
See how the enemy benefits us
Remember the potential goodness of the enemy
Repay hostility with kindness

Letting Go of Grudges and Resentment

Avoid cultivating grudges
Understand why others harm us
Remember our commonality with others
Forgive others

When Trust Is Betrayed

See the person as our supreme teacher
Inspect our unrealistic expectations
Rejoice in a positive past
Accept that change is universal
Recognize the nature of cyclic existence
Look at our situation from a wider perspective

The Snake of Envy

See the disadvantages of envy

Change our motivation to wishing others happiness

Don't envy what doesn't bring lasting happiness (or even what
does)

Rejoice that others are better than we are

Rejoice in others' good fortune and excellent qualities

Anger at Ourselves

Have love and compassion for ourselves

Focus on the positive

Value our good circumstances

Acknowledge our mistakes and laugh at ourselves

Accept ourselves as we are

Remember our Buddha potential

Aspire to change

Purify negativities

Cultivating Love and Compassion

See the advantages of a kind heart

Meditate on the kindness of others

Meditate on love

Understand compassion

Meditate on compassion

Meditate on taking and giving

Practice visualization and chanting meditations

Practice love and compassion in our lives

Helping Others Subdue Their Anger

Listen to friends who are angry

Do not take sides

Let go when we cannot help

Teach children to work with their anger

Be a good example

Love children when they are angry

Wisdom That Relaxes the Mind

Try to find the "I" that is angry
Free ourselves from anger completely

GLOSSARY

Anger
Based on an exaggeration or projection of negative qualities, an emotion that cannot endure an object, person, idea, etc. and wishes either to destroy or get away from it.

Attachment
Based on an exaggeration or projection of positive qualities, an emotion that clings to and craves its object—a person, idea, possession, position of status, etc.

Buddha
Any person who has purified all defilements and developed all good qualities. "The Buddha" refers to Shakyamuni Buddha, who lived over 2,500 years ago in India.

Buddha nature (Buddha potential)
The innate qualities of the mind enabling all beings to attain enlightenment.

Compassion
The wish for someone to be free from suffering.

Cyclic existence (samsara)
The cycle of constantly recurring problems in which we are caught due to ignorance.

Dharma

The Buddha's teachings. The cessations of suffering and its causes and the paths leading to them.

Disturbing attitudes and negative emotions

Attitudes and emotions, such as ignorance, attachment, anger, pride, jealousy, and closed-mindedness, that disturb our mental peace and propel us to act in ways harmful to ourselves and others.

Emptiness

The lack of independent or inherent existence. This is the ultimate nature, or reality, of all persons and phenomena.

Enlightenment (Buddhahood)

The state of a Buddha, i.e. the state of having forever eliminated all obscurations from the mindstream, and having developed our good qualities and wisdom to their fullest extent. All beings have the ability to attain enlightenment.

Ignorance

A mental factor that, unaware of the nature of reality, conceives people and phenomena to exist as independent entities unrelated to any other phenomenon.

Karma

Intentional action, which may be physical, verbal, or mental. Our actions leave imprints on our mindstreams, which bring about our experiences.

Lamrim

The Tibetan name for the gradual path to enlightenment, a step-by-step layout of the path.

Liberation

Freedom from cyclic existence through having eliminated the causes of suffering.

Love
The wish for someone to have happiness and its causes.

Mantra
A series of syllables consecrated by a Buddha and expressing the essence of the entire path to enlightenment. They are recited to concentrate and purify the mind.

Meditation
Habituating ourselves with positive attitudes and correct perspectives.

Mind
The experiential, cognitive part of living beings. Formless, the mind isn't made of atoms, nor is it perceivable through our five senses. It is mere clarity and awareness.

Mindstream
The continuity of the mind.

Purification practice
A four-step practice involving 1) regretting our mistake, 2) restoring the relationship by generating a positive attitude towards the one we harmed, 3) resolving to avoid the harmful action in the future, and 4) doing some sort of remedial behavior. This mitigates the force of our destructive actions.

Relative truth
The conventional existence of phenomena.

Relative world
The world of functioning, dependently arising things.

Refuge object
Those we turn to for spiritual guidance. For Buddhists, these are the Three Jewels—the Buddhas, Dharma, and Sangha.

FURTHER READING

Chodron, Thubten. *Buddhism for Beginners*. Ithaca: Snow Lion, 2001.

Chodron, Thubten. *Open Heart, Clear Mind*. Ithaca: Snow Lion, 1990.

Chodron, Thubten. *Taming the Monkey Mind*. Torrance: Heian, 1999.

Dalai Lama. *Healing Anger*. Ithaca: Snow Lion, 1997.

Dalai Lama. *Kindness, Clarity and Insight*. Ithaca: Snow Lion, 1984.

Dalai Lama. *Training the Mind*. Boston: Wisdom, 1999.

Dalai Lama and Howard C. Cutler. *The Art of Happiness: A Handbook for Living*. New York: Riverhead Books, 1998.

Dhammananda, K. Sri. *How to Live Without Fear and Worry*. Kuala Lumpur: Buddhist Missionary Society, 1989.

Dhammananda, K. Sri. *What Buddhists Believe*. Kuala Lumpur: Buddhist Missionary Society, 1987.

Dhammananda, K. Sri, ed. *The Dhammapada*. Kuala Lumpur: Sasana Abhiwurdhi Wardhana Society, 1988.

Dharmaraksita. *Wheel of Sharp Weapons*. Dharamsala, India: Library of Tibetan Works and Archives, 1981.

Dilgo Khyentse Rinpoche. *Enlightened Courage*. Ithaca: Snow Lion, 1993.

Epstein, Mark. *Thoughts Without a Thinker: Psychotherapy from a Buddhist Perspective*. New York: HarperCollins, 1995.

Epstein, Mark. *Going to Pieces Without Falling Apart: A Buddhist Perspective on Wholeness.* New York: Broadway Books, 1998.

Goldstein, Joseph. *The Experience of Insight.* Boston: Shambhala, 1987.

Goleman, Daniel, ed. *Healing Emotions: Conversation with the Dalai Lama on Mindfulness, Emotions and Health.* Boston: Shambhala, 1997.

Goleman, Daniel, et al. *Worlds in Harmony: Dialogues on Compassionate Action: His Holiness the Dalai Lama.* Berkeley: Parallax Press, 1991.

Greenberg, Mark, and Carol Kuché. Promoting Alternative Thinking Strategies (PATHS). http://www.psu.edu/dept/prevention/PATHS

Hanh, Thich Nhat. *Being Peace.* Berkeley: Parallax Press, 1987.

Khema, Ayya. *Being Nobody, Going Nowhere.* Boston: Wisdom, 1987.

Khema, Ayya. *Be an Island: The Buddhist Practice of Inner Peace.* Boston: Wisdom, 1999.

McDonald, Kathleen. *How to Meditate.* Boston: Wisdom, 1984.

Rabten, Geshe and Geshe Dhargyey. *Advice from a Spiritual Friend.* Boston: Wisdom, 1986.

Rinchen, Geshe Sonam and Ruth Sonam. *Thirty-seven Practices of Bodhisattvas.* Ithaca: Snow Lion, 1996.

Sparham, Gareth, trans. *Tibetan Dhammapada.* Boston: Wisdom, 1983.

Tegchok, Geshe Jampa. *Transforming the Heart: The Buddhist Way to Joy and Courage.* Ithaca: Snow Lion, 1999.

Tsongkhapa. *The Three Principal Aspects of the Path.* Howell, N.J.: Mahayana Sutra and Tantra Press, 1988.

Wangchen, Geshe. *Awakening the Mind of Enlightenment.* Boston: Wisdom, 1988.

Wilmot, William W. and Hocker, Joyce L. *Interpersonal Conflict.* New York: McGraw-Hill, 2001.

Yeshe, Lama Thubten. *Becoming Your Own Therapist.* Weston, MA: Lama Yeshe Wisdom Archives, 1998.

Yeshe, Lama Thubten. *Make Your Mind an Ocean*. Weston, MA: Lama Yeshe Wisdom Archives, 1999.

Zopa Rinpoche. *Door to Satisfaction*. Boston: Wisdom, 1994.

Zopa Rinpoche. *Transforming Problems: Utilizing Happiness and Suffering in the Spiritual Path*. Boston: Wisdom, 1987.